DAYTRIPS

—TO—

ARCHAEOLOGICAL
MEXICO

A Panoramic View of the Twelve Travel Routes

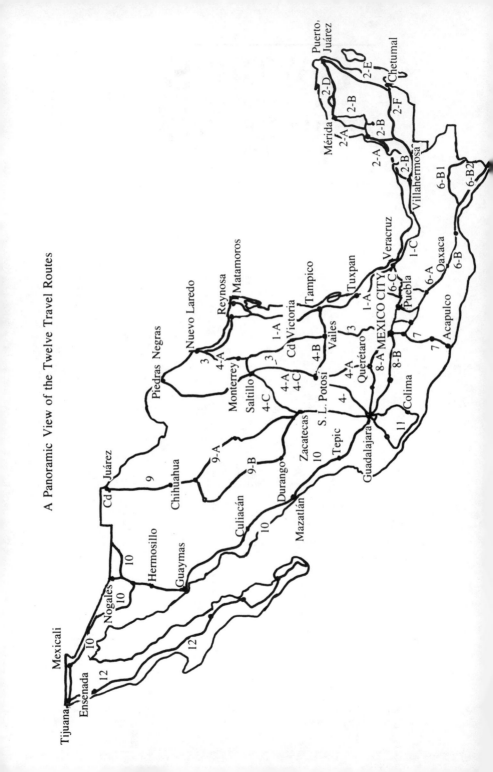

DAYTRIPS
—TO—
ARCHAEOLOGICAL MEXICO

by
Robert D. Wood

HASTINGS HOUSE
Book Publishers
MAMARONECK, NEW YORK

Originally published by Hastings House as
A Travel Guide to Archaeological Mexico
Copyright © 1979 by Robert D. Wood

This edition completely revised and updated
by the author and now published under the title
Daytrips to Archaeological Mexico
Copyright © 1991 by Robert D. Wood

ISBN 0–8038–9336–1
Library of Congress Catalog Card Number 91-074152

Distributed to the trade by Publishers Group West, Emeryville, CA

Printed in the United States of America

Preface

This book is an updated and schematically revised version of *A TRAVEL GUIDE TO ARCHAEOLOGICAL MEXICO* published twelve years ago. The purpose of that book was to help tourists who go in search of archaeological sites, captivated by the fascinating finds of the people who dedicate their time and talents to delving into the mysterious and long-lost past, and discovering new facts and artifacts which help piece together the lives of the inhabitants of the Americas before the arrival of the European invaders. This time is often referred to as Pre-Columbian (before Columbus) or Pre-Hispanic. Today's tourists are discoverers of what archaeologists have learned about Mexico's early cultures and the places where they developed.

Mexico offers the amateur archaeologist, the archaeology "buff" and the student of Pre-Hispanic history one of the most enriching and exciting vacations possible through trips to some of the many "ruins" scattered throughout this land of colorful contrasts where civilizations flourished before those of classical Greece and Rome. The country is unique in that it offers everything from cave dwellings to the remains of the sophisticated societies of the Aztecs and Mayas. Mexico is, in a sense, one vast museum. There are some 10,988 verified and officially recognized archaeological sites, and hundreds of unofficial ones. 126 of these are open to the public. Many of these sites were formerly unknown to tourists mainly because of the lack of roads.

This has changed dramatically, and the thirty-two states and Federal District of Mexico can now be reached by bus or automobile over 222,935 kilometers/139,334 miles of roads (throughout this guide "k" means kilometers and "m" miles). Many of the archaeological sites lie near these highways and are easily accessible. But as a Mexican Tourist Office publication states, they are "probably known only by archaeologists and nearby villagers and passed over by guidebooks," which usually mention only the long-known and outstanding sites like **Teotihuacán, Cholula** and **Chichén-Itzá**. Few if any mention **Ixtépete** right on the outskirts of Guadalajara, or **Dzibilchaltún**—only a few miles north of Mérida on a fine road—where people have been living since 2,000 B.C. There are also several sites where archaeological work is in progress and can be watched (e.g. **El Tajín** or **Tamuín**). However, most archaeological work is done between December and May, which is the "dry" season in most of

5

Mexico. Travelers in the summer months are not liable to find too many "digs" in progress. But new sites are constantly coming to light (e.g. **Cacaxtla**), and old ones being improved and made better known. This is the main reason why a new edition of the guide is necessary. It should be stated, however, that the book in no way pretends to offer extensive or exhaustive treatment of Mexican Pre-Hispanic cultures and archaeological sites. The purpose of this guide is to tell you how to get to these sites and offer a brief summary of information which will give an overview of the site and some of the more interesting facts about it.

Friends and other travelers have offered suggestions to improve a book they found useful. There are basically two, and this new edition includes both of them. The *Travel Guide* was directed originally and mainly to motorists. This work includes bus possibilities where it can (and the Metro in Mexico City), so that it becomes useful to more people.

Secondly, the five Parts of the original guide have been reduced to two. Part I offers some general archaeological and travel hints and information not found in the regular Mexican Tourist Office brochures and publications. In Part II, the information on the archaeological regions, on each site and on the people who lived there has been combined and coordinated with the various routes, eliminating the cross-referencing necessary before. Much of the information has also been updated. Since a lot can be learned from the archaeological collections in museums and they are usually well worth visiting, this book also mentions them by cities (some 25 have been added) and, whenever possible, gives some indication of their contents and the days/hours they are open. "Adm" means there is an admission fee. Many of these are small—one or two rooms. Don't be deceived by this. They often contain things not found anywhere else, especially if they are in small towns. Throughout the text, names in **bold-face** refer to archaeological sites, those in *italics* to Pre-Hispanic cultures. Measurements are generally given in meters (a meter equals 39 inches; 20 meters is 65 feet).

There are two basic ways to use this guide. One is to choose a destination (e.g. **Veracruz**) or specific site (**Mitla**) and look in the Index for the pages on which it can be found. By checking the route you can discover the sites along the way or determine the exact location of the site and how to get there. The other way is to read through the various routes and choose the one which appeals to you most. Almost all the sites indicated on the Mexican Tourist Office maps are included in this guide, plus many additional ones. Besides my own research and revisiting of many sites, information and assistance were given by several people. I would like to acknowledge particularly the gracious and invaluable help of Sra. Guadalupe Mastache Flores, the Assistant Director of Archaeological Studies in Mexico City, and Guadalupe Rojas Flores of the office of National Coordination of Organization, Information and Evaluation at the I.N.A.H., the personnel of the Information Office at the Ministry of Tourism (Mexico City) and in the various local tourist offices. Helpful information was also given by archaeologists Enrique Méndez (Mexico City), José M. Perea (Tamuín), Sergio Palacios (Campeche) and Jack Eaton (San Antonio). Thanks also to Dr. Jorge Chirinos Fano (Ecatepec), Bro. Ralph Neumann (Querétaro) and Bro. Carlos Villalobos (Mexico City) for their assistance. I owe special thanks to my sister, Mary Jean Wood, who proofread the whole manuscript for me.

At the suggestion of the editor, another new feature has been added which is found in Appendix 1—a listing of "daytrips," or sites which can be visited while remaining in one particular city and returning there for the night.

However you use this book it will help you in your adventures of seeking and finding easily accessible archaeological centers and even some which might challenge the more adventuresome. The experience is educational, enjoyable and unforgettable.

Contents

10   CONTENTS

Part I

GENERAL ARCHAEOLOGICAL AND TRAVEL INFORMATION

MEXICO'S EARLY HISTORY

Most of the well-known, excavated and restored archaeological sites in Mexico lie in what is known as Mesoamerica. The word means literally "middle America," and the region it refers to is, in fact, about the middle of the American continents. There is no absolute boundary for Mesoamerica, but the northern line runs diagonally from Tampico on the Gulf Coast to Culiacán on the Pacific, cutting more or less through the middle of Mexico. All of the southern part of Mexico, and the Yucatán peninsula, are included in Mesoamerica, along with the present-day countries of Belize, Guatemala, El Salvador and the western part of Honduras. It was in this area that most of the major Pre-Columbian cultures developed. There are some interesting ruins in northern Mexico also, but they are fewer and more widely scattered.

These Mexican cultures did not develop simultaneously, nor is it possible to establish an absolute chronology for all of the cultures, but historians and archaeologists have more or less agreed upon a broad chronology and the characteristics of each time period. There is a wonderful huge wall chart in the National Museum of Anthropology in Mexico City where you can see the whole thing at a glance.

The first period, called Prehistoric, ranges from 25,000 to 5,000 B.C. This is the age of the hunting-and-gathering groups, of stone tools and weapons, of a simple, nomadic life or cave dwelling. The beginnings of some agriculture may have come at the end of this first stage.

11

The second period, labeled Primitive, covers the time between 5,000 and 1,000 B.C. Some think that there were northward movements from Colombia, Ecuador or even Peru, mainly on rafts sailing up the Pacific. This brought about the introduction of certain pottery styles. Small villages began to form, and the early great culture, that of the *Olmecs*, had its beginnings. Very recently discoveries have been made in Belize which indicate that the roots of the *Maya* civilization may go back much farther than previously believed and even predate the other early cultures.

About 1,000 B.C. the Pre-classic or archaic era began. It saw the rise of the agrarian cultures in the Anáhuac valley, the beginnings of polytheism, the proliferation of clay figurines, the construction of the first pyramids and temples, and the invention of the calendar, and perhaps some forms of writing. This era closed around 200 B.C. From that date until about 400 A.D. the Formative (or Protoclassic) period was taking place. By this time the *Olmecs* were in Veracruz and Tabasco, and other urban centers began to grow. A hierarchical religion developed, with a ruling sacerdotal class in charge of government, public works, commerce, intellectual and artistic accomplishments and religion as such. Social systems and classes emerged. Pottery-making technology greatly improved.

The fifth period, or Classic Age, extended from 400 to 900. Great civilizations flourished, especially those of **Teotihuacán, El Tajín, Monte Albán, Cholula**, and the *Maya* centers like **Bonampak, Edzná, Palenque, Río Bec** and **Yaxchilán**. There was extensive cultural and commercial interchange. About the middle of this period, the northern fringe of Mesoamerica began to experience raids and attacks by warlike nomadic groups from the north. They had the bow and arrow, enabling them to wound and kill without hand-to-hand combat. Migrations and general population movements brought about the foundation of new centers, and a kind of domino effect of emigration. The inability of the priestly caste to solve these problems, and perhaps their domineering ways, brought about a decline in the theocratic centers.

The Post-Classic age began around 900 and lasted until the arrival of the Europeans. Military groups like the *Toltecs* extended their kingdoms. Walled and fortified cities were built. On the Yucatán peninsula, the Itzás and Xius tried to revive the *Maya* civilization and **Chichén-Itzá, Mayapán** and **Uxmal** formed a league which lasted about two centuries. It was an age of alliances between chiefdoms, and of political confederations. From 1200 on, the Anáhuac valley became the scene of the rise of many city-states, and of the infiltration of the *Chichimec* groups, one of which—the Tenochas—would eventually subjugate all of the others and become the *Aztec* empire. During all of this time, there was a constant evolution in economic specialization, juridical systems, commerce and trade, social organizations, the arts, religious thought and practice, and technological "know-how." It is no surprise that archaeologists find Mesoamerica a fascinating region in which to work, and tourists are constantly visiting these vestiges of Mexico's early cultures.

WHEN TO TRAVEL

Many people do not have much choice as to when they may travel, since it is tied in with the vacation time they can get from their work. For them, where to travel might be more important than when. The two are somewhat tied together, however, and are based on Mexico's geography and climate. The fact that Mexico is so mountainous means that even though most of the country lies in the tropics, the temperature is often a lot lower than it would normally be, because of the altitude. Only at the lower altitudes or at sea level does it get "stifling" and very hot, particularly during the summer months. Climate-wise, winter travel in the southern half of Mexico is excellent almost everywhere. It's more like spring than winter. In the north, however, winter travel is usually a bit brisk and chilly, and even the "tropical" beaches are deserted.

Along with geography and climate, another important consideration in deciding when to travel is the question of weather. In Mexico, there are rains from May to December. The amount of rainfall varies, of course, in the different areas of the country. It rains more often and harder in the southern portions, and in the more tropical lowland areas. Many of the off-the-beaten-path sites become inaccessible because of rural roads which turn into mud and often have long-standing puddles which are difficult to cross. However, most of the major sites have all-weather roads leading to them and can be visited all year around. You may have trouble getting some pictures, though mornings tend to be clear and fairly bright, and now and then even a little sun will slip through the scattered clouds. You can always use the rainy afternoons that come along for visiting museums, souvenir shopping or just general relaxing.

Another thing to keep in mind are the national holidays (listed in most Mexican Tourist Office brochures). It's pretty frustrating to arrive somewhere on a Friday and find out that the banks and public offices are closed because it's a holiday, and Saturday and Sunday are coming up. Generally business goes on as usual on the religious feast days (except December 12, Christmas, and January 6) but the national civic holidays bring out the "closed" signs. There are ten of them, also listed in the above-mentioned brochures, along with a lot of local feast days. Keep in mind, also, that hotel rooms are very hard to find in any of the seaside resort areas during the holiday seasons (Christmas, Easter, Carnival days). It is also important for archaeology-minded vacationers to remember that throughout Mexico, most museums and even some sites are closed on Mondays, and are likely to be closed on holidays also. In Mexico City there is a service called "Infotur." Dial 525-9380 and ask (in English) whatever you want to know. Most of the time your question(s) will be answered.

DOCUMENTS

Visitors to Mexico need a tourist permit which they can get from any Mexican Tourist Office or Consulate in the States, or from the airline they use to go to Mexico by showing either a) a valid passport, b) a birth certificate or c) a voter's registration card. The permits can also be obtained at the various border crossings. It saves time to have one already filled out. If you enter Mexico with a car, you must have the title to it, or a notorized permission from the legal owner authorizing you to take it to Mexico. Mexican auto insurance is optional, but highly recommended (U.S. insurance is not valid in Mexico).

TRAVELING IN MEXICO

1. By car. Before deciding to take your car to Mexico, you will naturally have a lot of questions you want answered. The following will include some of those things.

What about the roads? Mexico has a good highway system, and 98,574k/61,608m of them are black top and generally kept in reasonably good condition. There are also some freeways and toll roads which compare to those found in this country. They are marked "Cuota." Toll roads are fairly expensive (about .14 a mile). Toll-free roads which frequently run parallel to the toll roads are marked "Libre." For the most part, highways and secondary roads are all-weather roads, but they are generally only two lanes which are not divided. Suggestion: don't try "short-cuts" you might figure out from a map before inquiring about road conditions. And please, don't expect to be able to drive right up to the pyramid steps on a smooth road. Every site requires a good bit of walking and some roads are very primitive and require careful, slow driving, but you will be told this whenever it's the case.

One thing you may miss are the rest areas common in this country. There are none along the Mexican highways. You may just have to make your own "comfort station" off the road somewhere.

Is driving safe? Most driving is as safe as the driver makes it. There is a particular hazard in Mexico: wandering animals. Along most of the highways you'll find animals grazing. Some are tethered; many are not. A donkey might take the notion to start across the highway just as you come zooming along. About all you can do is keep a watchful eye and drive at a speed at which you have complete control of your car. If at all possible, don't drive at night. Animals are usually dark-colored to begin with, and at night it's almost impossible to see them until it's too late. You can miss a pothole in the road, too. Another precaution: don't pull off the road for a quick snooze or nap in any area that is not populated, especially if you are driving alone. That tempts would-be car thieves and robbers.

Is there a speed limit? Yes. On highways the maximum speed is usually 100k/62mph. Most cities reduce speed to 30 kph in the heart of town. All distances in Mexico are indicated in kilometers. This guide generally indicates both kilometers and miles, but there is also a conversion table in Appendix 3.

What about gas and oil? There is only one "brand" of gas in Mexico: Pemex (an abbreviation for Petroleros Mexicanos). For cars, there are two kinds of gasoline. The silver-and-green colored pumps dispense the equivalent of U.S. "extra," lead-free gas (they are marked "Magna sin"). This is sold by the liter, which is a fraction more than a quart. The blue pumps, labeled "Nova" or "Extra Nova" dispense Mexico's "regular" gasoline. For the best performance, especially if a lot of mountain driving is involved, stick with the "extra." You'll see red pumps at many of the Pemex stations, also. These have diesel fuel. It's a very wise precaution to use a gas cap with a lock. Make sure the station attendant turns the gauges back to zero. Some like to make extra pesos by "forgetting."

When you need oil, there are several good brands. Faja de Oro, 10-4-SAE or Multigrade are among the best.

Foreign credit cards are not accepted at Mexican gasoline stations, and traveler's checks will sometimes be refused. Be prepared to pay in cash. In fact, gas stations are a good place to get peso bills of the bigger denominations changed.

A few other hints:

Have your entry permit handy at all times. You will be stopped along the way at immigration check points, usually about 14k/9m from the border.

Keep a little change box handy (50, 100 and even 1000 peso coins) mainly for parking meters, toll roads, toll bridges, and for children who will invariably offer to watch or wash your car while you are at the ruins. Accept these offers. They cost very little and a refusal might result in a deflated or slashed tire.

Don't forget that water boils at a lower temperature in the mountains. Check your radiator more frequently, and even carry along some extra water.

Never leave your car unlocked, or on the street overnight. Choose a motel or a hotel with garage facilities, even if it's a little more inconvenient.

Mexican Tourist Office maps and brochures indicate all of the common road signs. One that frequently does not appear, however, is the sign for city traffic. In most cities of Mexico, the downtown section streets are one way. This is usually indicated by an arrow with the word "tránsito" or "circulación" in it, or simply by the arrow itself. They are often painted on the walls of the buildings at the corner, and sometimes you have to look a bit to find them. As a general rule, streets alternate so that traffic goes the same direction every other block. One sign of importance to users of this guide is the blue-bordered sign with a three-tiered truncated pyramid in the center. This indicates an archaeological zone with notable structures. Usually the sign appears one or two kilometers before the site itself, and again at or near the ruins or reconstructions.

If you need help, think of the Mexican Tourist Office first. There is a Hotline in Mexico City (250-0123). The addresses for each city are given in the information leaflets and there is usually someone who speaks English. Many travelers to Mexico do not know that twice a day over most of the highways small green trucks carry two English-speaking men who are constantly on the lookout for motorists in trouble, and especially tourists. These trucks are compact gas stations, garages and first-aid units all rolled into one. The men will assist in repairing any mechanical difficulty, or will radio for a tow truck if repair is not possible. They charge nothing for their services and sell gas, oil or automotive parts at cost price. These amiable, efficient helpers are known as "Los Angeles Verdes"—The Green Angels. If something happens on the highway that you can't take care of yourself, just sit tight and sooner or later the Green Angels will come along to help you.

For travelers to Mexico City there is a new and very important change. All cars, including those of foreigners, are forbidden to circulate one day a week, according to the last number of the license plates. The restrictions are as follows:

Monday—plates ending in 5 or 6
Tuesday—plates ending in 7 or 8
Wednesday—plates ending in 3 or 4
Thursday—plates ending in 1 or 2
Friday—plates ending in 9 or 0

If your car license plate is 234 XYZ, or 621 773, you can't drive in Mexico City on Wednesdays. So, plan accordingly.

2. By bus. In Mexico City there are four main bus terminals, one for each of the cardinal points, or directions. All four can be easily reached by the metro system. The north station (buses to and through all the cities on roads leading to the Mexico-U.S. border) is on metro line 5 which can be connected to at La Raza station (on line 3). The east station (to the Gulf Coast) is at the San Lázaro metro stop (line 1). The south station (to Oaxaca, the Guatemala border, Acapulco) is at the end of metro line 2 at Tasqueña. The buses to Morelia, Guadalajara and the Pacific Coast leave from the west station at metro stop Observatorio on line 1. Below is a chart showing the services which can be found at the various stations.

	North	East	South	West
cafeteria, food stands	x	x	x	x
drug store	x	x		x
hotel information	x		x	
luggage lockers		x	x	x
money exchange	x			
newspapers, magazines	x	x	x	x
post office	x	x	x	x
souvenirs	x	x	x	x
telegraph	x	x		x
tourist agencies			x	
tourist information	x	x	x	

All the major cities have bus terminals and you can cover Mexico fairly easily by "leap-frogging" from place to place, though there are also long-distance lines.

Bus fares are relatively inexpensive and the bus stations are always crowded. Most people buy tickets for the next bus out. Reservations are possible one day in advance in some stations, but are not common. In some cases tickets may be purchased a day in advance. It's mostly "play by ear" for bus travel. Usually there is no problem and there are frequent departures to many destinations (e.g. Mexico City to Querétaro or Celaya every half hour). Most buses are comfortable, but have little overhead room. Large bags have to be stored below. Except on very long trips there is usually no lavatory on the buses, but they do make rest stops occasionally. Several companies may go to the same destination, and there are price differences, especially if they offer the "deluxe" service (a lavatory and beverages on board). When you are boarding a bus, watch your wallet or purse! In fact, it is best not to carry money in the usual places. Don't wear expensive watches or jewelry. If someone asks you for the time, don't just hold your arm out. "Snatch-thieving" has unfortunately become more prevalent and bus and subway travelers are prime targets. A little prudence and common sense is all that is needed and things will go fine. Never leave your luggage unattended in a bus station. Keep cameras and camera equipment out of sight if possible.

Sometimes at the border towns Mexicans may ask you if you will carry a package for them. Just refuse politely. They are probably trying to get something past the customs officials who tend to check their fellow Mexicans rather thoroughly and foreigners rather cursorily. All of this may sound a bit paranoid, but it's simply a question of "better safe than sorry." Why have a trip spoiled because of something you hadn't thought of?

3. Using city transportation. While in Mexico City, leave your car at the hotel or motel and use the Metro or bus systems. The Metro is attractively clean, efficient and incredibly cheap (it's a good idea to buy several tickets at a time; lines are sometimes long). You can transfer from one line to another at no extra cost (look for the word "correspondencia") and ride from one end of Mexico City to the other for less than ten cents. Every station has clearly indicated "Dirección . . ." (heading toward . . .) with the name of the last station on the line. There are charts in the stations and in each car of the train to show the stops. If you want to go to **Tlaltelolco**, for instance, you would take line **3**, Dirección "Indios Verdes," and get off at the Tlaltelolco stop. You will have a few blocks to walk. City buses going north on Reforma will also take you within easy walking distance. As you travel the Metro, notice the stations. Some of them (like Bellas Artes) are very artistically arranged and really beautiful. They put some of our U.S. graffiti-filled stations and train cars to shame.

Like the buses, the Metro stations are jammed a good part of the day, but the crowd moves along steadily. Try to avoid traveling between 6–8 a.m. and 5–7 p.m. Pickpockets are regular riders (some spend the whole day riding back and forth!), so keep money and valuables in well protected places. A lot of vendors board the trains and hawk their wares for a few stops, and there are musicians and beggars. Don't feel obliged to contribute to any of them.

TAKING THE ESSENTIALS

Lists of what to take with you on a trip depend pretty much on the individual's needs and tastes. However, it's almost an axiom that most travelers take too much. There are some things, though, that you might wish you had if you haven't thought to bring them along. Here are a few suggestions:

> a.) comfortable, low-heeled walking shoes or basketball shoes or sneakers. At most archaeological sites you have to do a good bit of walking, and sometimes some climbing, and the terrain is frequently rugged.
>
> b.) a raincoat and/or umbrella if you travel between May and December.
>
> c.) a sweater, jacket or light coat for the mountains almost all year around.
>
> d.) an extra pair of your regular prescription glasses, especially if they are not shatter-proof.
>
> e.) insect repellant for the tropical areas, especially Chiapas and Yucatán.
>
> f.) sun tan lotion, if you burn easily, or are going to the tropical regions.
>
> g.) a box of Kleenex or small packs of facial tissue. You'll find a dozen uses for them.

h.) prescription medicines you take regularly. Suggestions for medicines for stomach and diarrhea problems are given under Eating and Drinking.

i.) a small sewing kit.

j.) a small flashlight.

k.) a washcloth or two; only the deluxe hotels have them.

LODGING

All hotels, motels and motor courts have rates authorized by the Mexican government. These rates depend upon the condition of the room, its furnishings, the conveniences, etc. The authorized rates should be on display in the room itself, and at the front desk. At certain times of the year, hotels are allowed to increase rates by ten or fifteen per cent (the weeks before and after Easter, the Christmas season and the Carnival days). In southern Mexico along the Pacific coast and along the Caribbean coast of Yucatán December to April is the "high" season, and hotels usually charge considerably more, especially in the well-known resort areas.

Hotels used to be rated by categories (AA, A and B), but most are now classified by "stars." Five-star and four-star hotels are deluxe and very expensive (many of them belong to major international chains like Hilton, Holiday Inn or Sheraton); three-star hotels have good service and often include extras like TV, swimming pool and air conditioning. Two-star hotels are clean, neat and usually comfortable, but have nothing fancy. Things are plain and simple, but sufficient. Almost all hotels have hot water. The fixtures, however, may be reversed from what we are used to in this country. Because American fixtures were used in many hotels, the "H" stands for "helado" (cold) and the "C" for "caliente" (hot). Electrical current is the same as in the States, but most hotels ask you not to plug in heavy appliances (e.g. hot plates). Appendix 2 offers some motels/hotels for the budget-minded.

EATING AND DRINKING

People's "insides" are as different as their faces and features, and it is not true that "What's good for the goose is good for the gander." Only you know your eating habits and what agrees and disagrees with you, but there are some basic hints which can keep people comfortably healthy while traveling. More problems come from excessive worry about Mexican microbes than from the food or liquid itself. So much has been written and said about "traveler's diarrhea," known to Mexican travelers as "Montezuma's revenge," that people go to Mexico almost expecting to get sick. There's no need to. I think my stomach is as normal as anyone else's, and in all the times I have traveled to Mexico, I have never been struck by this dreaded calamity. I'll tell you what my secrets are, and maybe you will find them useful.

Central Mexico averages from 5,000 to 7,500 ft. in altitude. You have to give your body a chance to adapt. Rushing around from place to place can upset your stomach and system as much as the wrong food or water. Slow down a bit; take a nap if you feel tired.

Any sudden change of diet or of eating and drinking habits can disrupt the internal flora and the routine your system has set up, so the first rule is to make the change gradually. If you drive, take along a thermos or a jug of water so you are drinking the water you are used to, and add to it the first day with bottled water or the purified water you will find in most hotels in huge glass jugs, usually in the hallways or general public areas. Don't drink the tap water, even where they say it is safe to do so. If you do not find bottled water in your room, ask for "agua purificada" (ah-gwa poo-ree-fee-cah'-dah). Or try some type of soda. "Tehuacán" (tay-wah-kahn') has both bottled water and several types of fruit-tasting drinks. "Peñafiel" (pain-ya-fee-el') is another common brand name. "Sidral" (see-drahl') is a refreshing apple juice type drink. Names like Sprite, Seven-Up, Fanta (but say fahn'-tah), Coca Cola and Pepsi are readily understood everywhere. And, of course, there's always beer (beer is "cerveza"—sair-vay'-sah), but remember that alcohol takes effect more quickly at the higher altitudes. Don't drink milk except in the better class hotels and restaurants (unless it is already in cartons). An exception can be made for coffee with milk, very commonly served for breakfast, because the milk is boiled. *Avoid ice cubes!* I think this is where most people meet their downfall. Most of the time the cubes are made with tap water, and the amoebas are not frozen. Amoebas are the cause of most of the diarrhea problems of travelers in Mexico. For the same reason, don't buy a "raspado" which is grated ice with a fruit syrup poured over it. If you want something cold, order one of the bottled drinks mentioned above and say "helada" (eh-lah'-dah, cold) with it. When you order fresh fruit juice (perfectly safe and usually delicious), ask for it "sin hielo" (seen yay'-low), without ice.

In regard to foods, omelet is a good dish to fall back on. No problem with roasted meat or chicken. There is always lots of rice (ah-ros') and while it may not always be too savory it is always safe. Avoid fresh, uncooked vegetables like lettuce or tomatoes except in first class hotels and restaurants. Another pretty good bet is soup (so'-pah). The water has been boiled a fairly long time, and Mexicans have a way of concocting very tasty combinations. If you're an ice cream lover, you'll have to be careful where you buy. Ice cream parlors, similar to those in this country, are O.K. Don't buy from vendors on the street unless they are peddling name brands (e.g. Holanda, Danesa 33, Yom-Yom, Bambinos). Another wonderful thing to rely on are the bread and pastry shops—safe and delicious. (So who's counting calories on vacation?)

Eat lightly at first. It's better to nibble safe things several times a day than stuff yourself at the first evening meal. Meal hours for breakfast and lunch are the same as in the U.S., but the evening meal is later. The afternoon snack, around 4:00, is a universal custom. There's nothing like a refreshing drink and a piece of pie after a long day at the ruins!

But suppose that in spite of all your precautions, you do get an upset stomach, or an attack of diarrhea. You can be prepared by taking some medicines with you. Physicians prescribe different things like Tigan for upset stomach or Lo-Motil for diarrhea. But there are non-prescription drugs you can get, also. Those suggested here have been recommended by a doctor in whom I have the fullest confidence. For the stomach: Alka-Selzer or Pepto-Bismol. For diarrhea: Imodium. If you do get diarrhea don't stop eating. Just eat lightly and carefully. Chances are that within 24 hours your condition will return to normal.

BUYING AND PAYING FOR THINGS

The Mexican monetary unit is the peso (pay'-so) which is divided into 100 centavos. The smaller coins (five and ten centavos) are rarely seen any more. 100 centavo coins are used for the telephone and for parking meters.

The Mexican peso sign is like the U.S. dollar sign, except that there is one line through the S instead of two. Sometimes the U.S. dollar sign is used, but it is followed by the letters M.N. (moneda nacional—national currency). If these letters are missing, then the prices quoted are in U.S. dollars, and this is often done for tourists.

It is almost impossible to cash personal checks, and sometimes in rural areas even traveler's checks will not be accepted. Credit cards are sometimes accepted, but don't count on using them frequently. It's better to have a ready supply of Mexican bills, if possible. Don't change money with strangers on the streets. Use a bank (9:00–1:30, M-F) or a "Casa de cambio" (money exchange house). Exchange houses do not usually ask for personal identification; banks always do.

Haggling over prices is a time-honored institution in Mexican markets, and no shopkeeper expects you to pay the price quoted except in department stores or supermarkets. You can bargain in most souvenir shops, too. One of the nice features of shopping in Mexico is that you pay the exact price agreed upon. There are no extra sales taxes or hidden charges. However, there is a 15% surtax in hotels and restaurants (some hotels include it when they quote the price of the room). On the other hand, you will seldom get a sales slip, so unless you keep track yourself, you'll never know how much you spent for what. Most shops are open from 9:00 a.m. to 7:00 p.m. though some close down for the afternoon siesta break, especially in the summer, but they will stay open until 8:00 or 9:00 p.m.

At archaeological sites, especially the more frequently visited ones, you will often be approached by men and boys who will offer to sell you "genuine" artifacts. They will do this furtively and make it look like a secret transaction, because to sell real artifacts would be a serious violation of the law. In some instances, and particularly in out-of-the-way places, the artifacts might really be old or Pre-Columbian. Most frequently they will be clay heads, figurines, or spindle-whorls. But beware! Unless you are an expert, or have actually seen the object taken from the ground at a dig, assume that it is not genuine. And remember that it is a violation of the law to bring any really valuable objects into the U.S. Besides, a person really devoted to archaeology would much prefer to see the objects remain in Mexico, since they are a part of its national patrimony.

TOURIST GUIDES

Theoretically, only persons authorized by the Mexican Tourist Office are allowed to act as guides. These persons must carry their credentials in the form of an identification card which they are supposed to show, even if not requested to. Authorized guides and driver-guides can be found at many of the multiple-star hotels. There are not many authorized guides at the sites themselves, but you will frequently find people (including young boys) willing to show you around and tell you the "historical facts" about the place, sometimes in halting English. My personal experience has been that these "facts" are often inaccurate, and more myth than truth. One of my favorite tricks is to ask "Habla francés?" (Do you speak French?) and the answer will surely be "no." Then I throw up my hands, shrug my shoulders and walk off. Almost any other language (except English) will work, too, since few people at the sites are bilingual or multilingual. With the background and information provided in this guide you will probably get a lot more out of your visit if you just wander around on your own. It should be noted that Mexico City and some other cities have tours which are fine for sightseeing, especially if your time in a given place is limited. They will take you to some of the archaeological spots nearby, or even arrange two or three day trips, but they don't pretend to be Pre-Columbian experts.

SOME SPECIAL CUSTOMS

Life moves at a different pace in Mexico; it is much more leisurely. This is one of the great joys of visiting Mexico. There is no "busy beat of time." True, traffic moves as though every car were an ambulance on call, but the theory behind that is why waste time on the street when you can be enjoying something elsewhere?

Businesses often close down between 1:00 and 4:00, especially in the summer, but like the shops may remain open fairly late. Don't expect things to happen on precision time. Learn to mosey, meander, meditate and sort of "drift" with the atmosphere. There's a lot of elasticity in Mexican living, and almost everything is "mas o menos" (more or less). Mexicans are not lazy; they just refuse to get uptight about such a secondary thing as time.

They are also much "warmer" and more outgoing than most Americans. They shake hands constantly, even with people they do not know very well. A five-minute conversation is sufficient to be called "amigo" thereafter. Don't be surprised to see men embracing on the street or walking along with their arms over one another's shoulders. The "abrazo" (hug) is a common greeting for friends or men who know each other fairly well. Women also shake hands with strangers, but the woman should offer her hand first. All women are addressed as "señorita" (miss) unless you know for sure that the woman is married, in which case it is "señora." This includes waitresses, hotel clerks, maids, etc., even if they are obviously elderly.

Smoking is still widespread and accepted in Mexico. There are no "no smoking" areas in most restaurants, for instance, though smoking is prohibited in the Metro stations and trains, and on most surface transportation. To ask someone to extinguish a cigarette would be considered very rude. Just move somewhere else.

One custom that sometimes shocks visitors is the fact that men (and sometimes even women) will relieve themselves in public, in the corner of a building or near a tree or billboard. Like time, urinating is a fact of life, so why get disturbed about it? In rural areas, younger children often run around naked, particularly in the more tropical regions, and older people bathe in the rivers, mainly because they have no facilities in their homes. Just accept these things as "normal."

Men do not wear shorts. Mexicans have learned to accept or at least tolerate men tourists who do wear them in certain beach resorts, but it would be considered offensive to do so in Mexico City or even Veracruz. In many places women are still expected to wear some sort of head covering when they enter a church, where very short skirts are still considered totally out of place.

There is no daylight saving time in Mexico. Baja California and the Pacific Coast states to Nayarit have U.S. Pacific and Rocky Mountain time; the rest of the country is on U.S. Central Standard Time. Bus schedules, theater showings and public functions and offices all use the 24-hour clock. Some stores close, for instance, from 14.00 to 16.00 (2 to 4 p.m.); "light and sound" shows start at 20.00 (8 p.m.).

Need a quick reference? 0.01 to 0.59 (12:01–12:59 a.m.); 1.00 to 12.00 would be the same as our morning hours. Then: 13.00 (1 p.m.); 14.00 (2 p.m.); 15.00 (3 p.m.); 16.00 (4 p.m.); 17.00 (5 p.m.); 18.00 (6 p.m.); 19.00 (7 p.m.); 20.00 (8 p.m.); 21.00 (9 p.m.); 22.00 (10 p.m.); 23.00 (11 p.m.); 24.00 (midnight).

Part II

TWELVE TRAVEL ROUTES

Route 1: The Gulf Coast

The Gulf Coast route is one of the easiest and most pleasant drives in Mexico. It divides somewhat naturally into two parts: the border to Veracruz, and Veracruz to Villahermosa.

1-A: THE BORDER TO VERACRUZ (992 OR 1240K/619 OR 775M)

The main artery for this trip is highway 180. It begins at Brownsville/Matamoros as highway 101. Highways 2 and 97 from McAllen/Reynosa, or Laredo/Nuevo Laredo join it. All of the Mexican cities have bus terminals with various choices of companies which have service to the major cities on this route: Tampico, Tuxpan, Poza Rica and Veracruz (Autotransportes de Oriente—ADO—is the most reliable, but there are Transportes Frontera, Tres Estrellas, Transportes del Norte, Omnibus de México from Reynosa; the first three from Nuevo Laredo; and Transportes del Norte and ADO from Matamoros).

Highway 180 separates from 101 about 48k/30m south of San Fernando. The sign reads "Soto La Marina." This road saves about 177k/111m and obviates the necessity of going through Ciudad Victoria and Ciudad Mante to get to Tampico. Although this portion of the route passes through country which is filled with known sites, mainly of the *Huastecs*, there are no accessible archaeological areas along the way. The first place you can visit is the little museum in Ciudad Madero, which lies between Tampico and the gulf. The road to that town branches off highway 180 just outside the north end of Tampico. It is called Ejercito Mexicano. Follow this all the way into town to where it becomes Sarabia street. Go three blocks and then turn left for one block to 1 de Mayo where the Technológico (Technological School) is located. In the main building, at the far end of the first floor to your right (you are still outside, really, in a kind of portico) there is a small museum (Mon-Fri, 9–5; Sat, 9–3). The displays are simple, but they offer various authentic aspects of the *Huastec* culture. Souvenir explanatory books are available in both English and Spanish. There is regular bus service (marked "Madero" or "Tampico-Playa") to Ciudad Madero from Tampico. Board the bus on Juárez street. You can get off right at the Technológico.

The *Huastecs* lived mainly along the Gulf Coast of Mexico, from the Río Grande (or Río Bravo) in the north to the Cazones river in Veracruz in the south, though they also spread into the mountain regions of present-day Veracruz, San Luis Potosí and even

27

Querétaro. The remote origins of this group go back to the caves of Tamaulipas and Nuevo León which they inhabited as early as 10,000 B.C. but their language shows possible Maya origins.

The second phase of their development was the formation into groups between 1100 and 600 B.C. in such places as Ponce, Aguilar, Tantoc, La Noria and Tambalón. During this time they were strongly influenced by the *Olmecs*. Between 600 B.C. and 200 A.D. they began to establish a cultural center at Pánuco where two distinct stages of development can be identified. With the rise and growth of **El Tajín** between 200 and 650, the Huastec culture advanced rapidly. Some impact came from other groups, particularly the *Totonacs*, though they managed to hold onto their own territory and cultural traits, particularly in the Pánuco area and at their great ceremonial center of **Tamuín**.

In 1467 they fought the *Aztecs* successfully, but they were eventually forced to pay tribute. They were first discovered by the Spaniards sailing the gulf coast in 1519, and Cortés himself visited the area in 1522.

One of the greatest influences in Pre-Columbian Mexico, the worship of Quetzalcoatl, may have begun with the Huastecs. The round structures dedicated to him as the wind god first appeared in the Veracruz region. Interestingly enough, the houses of the people themselves were circular, and the ceramics were sphere-shaped. The Huastecs traded with **Teotihuacán**, and a Huastec princess married the founder of **Tenayuca**, a city-state in central Mexico.

The Huastecs practiced cranial deformation, filed and blackened their teeth, and dyed their hair yellow. Ornamentation with feathers and shells was widespread. Several of the early Spanish chroniclers present a rather bad portrait of the Huastecs, depicting them as generally rude and given to sexual license (and perversion) and drunkenness. Whatever their cultural flaws may have been, the Huastecs did achieve a fairly high standard in art and craftsmanship, though their architecture was never as imposing as that of other cultures.

If your time and schedule permit, you can visit one of the main Huastec centers, **Tamuín**, which is located about 122k/70m west of Tampico off highway 70 (see Route 4-B). Buses from Tampico to Ciudad Valles (or beyond) go through the town. The "Vencedor" bus from Ciudad Valles passes by the ruins about once every hour. If you miss it you'll have to hike the 3 miles to the ruins—and back! Unfortunately the remains of pyramids in Colonia las Flores and Altamira, both near Tampico, have been destroyed (there are sketches of them in the Ciudad Madero museum).

To continue south on highway 180 from Tampico, follow Aduana street north through town. It will take you to the bridge which crosses the Pánuco river (be prepared to pay about $4.00 toll). Once across the river, you continue on past several small villages. About 11k/7m from Tampico you will come to Tampico Alto. The road to your left leads to the town. Follow it (watch out for the enormous speed bumps!) to the village church. Walk through the church yard to the right. You will find a museum of one large room (Tue-Sun, 8–1; 2–6; if closed go to the parish rectory). It contains several showcases of figurines and pottery, and a center row of fine stone sculptures, almost all *Huastec*. It is an interesting complement to the Ciudad Madero museum.

There are "colectivos" (marked "Isleta") from Héroes del Cañonero street (at the foot of Juárez street) in Tampico. They will take you to the ferry to cross the river. On the other side you get the "colectivo" marked "Tampico Alto."

193k/120m farther on you come to Tuxpan (sometimes with "m" instead of "n"). Follow the riverside boulevard to the main plaza, go left one block to Juárez and left again for three blocks to Plaza Juárez. You may have to park on some side street. The new museum is located on the west side of the plaza (Tue-Sat, 9–5, Adm).

Leaving Tuxpan you cross the river which was the boundary between the Huastecs and the *Totonacs*.

The *Totonacs* originally inhabited the mountain regions of eastern Puebla. In the tenth century, they were displaced by some of the roving *Toltec* groups, and moved toward the gulf coast, establishing centers at Ahuilizapan, Cuetlachtlán, Cuauhtochco (Huatusco), Misantla, Jalapa, Quiahuitzlán and **Cempoala**. They eventually took over most of the gulf coast territory between Veracruz and the Pánuco river. They incorporated **El Tajín** into their empire, and made **Cempoala** the capital of it. In 1469 this city was taken by the Aztecs under Moctezuma I and the Totonac empire became a tribute state. When Cortés arrived in 1519, the Totonacs at first battled against the Spaniards, but steel armor, cannons, horses and Spanish valor were too much for them and **Cempoala** fell to the foreigners. Cortés convinced them that he could liberate them from the terrible tribute (sacrificial victims) exacted by the *Aztecs*, and the Totonacs joined the Spanish forces to march against **Tenochtitlán**. Cortés, however, first toppled their idols and made them promise to give up their "abominable practices," including human sacrifice. Officially, human sacrifice was offered every three years, but in practice it was done more frequently, especially with children. Cultural traits of the Totonacs included cranial deformation, tatooing, wearing lip discs, "eternal" fires burning in the temples, and burial of the dead in rock-walled graves under their houses which were made of cane and roofed with straw.

Aztec subjugation kept the Totonac empire from expanding, and Spanish domination brought it to an end, especially since Veracruz became a major city and the principal port of New Spain (as Mexico was known in colonial times).

About 34k/21m from Tuxpan on highway 180 you will come to Tihuatlán. One kilometer farther on a paved road to the right leads to **Castillo del Teayo**, about 10k/7m into the hills. There is another road to Teayo via Zapotillo about 7k/4m farther down the highway, but it is a longer distance (about 22k/14m) to the pyramid.

Castillo del Teayo (kah-steel'-yo dell tay-eye-'yo) is really a misnomer. The Spaniards frequently dubbed any large architectural structure such as a pyramid or fortress a "castle." This fine monument and the surrounding area were studied by J. García Payón, particularly in 1950 and 1952. The actual town was established in 1872, but the single central pyramid was probably first a *Totonac* structure, later taken over by the *Toltecs* after the fall of **Tula**. Some archaeologists, in fact, consider it of Toltec origin. One archaeological opinion dates it at 815 A.D. The structure covers 576 square meters and is 13 meters high. It is built on a small foundation platform which has three levels with slanting walls. A monumental staircase covers the greater part of the front side. Several statues and stelae, found in the vicinity, now stand around the base of the pyramid. There are representations of Quetzalcoatl, of the god of corn, of Tlaloc, the god of rain, Xipe Totec, the flower god, and others. Some stelae have calendar glyphs on them. The former temple on top is replaced by a small room which houses a bell, still used for community purposes. There is a museum near the pyramid.

Continuing south on 180, the next archaeological site comes just after Poza Rica. Near the east end of town at the first major intersection a sign indicates turn right to **El Tajín**. You will go past the huge PEMEX complex. At the end, a very rough blacktop road (left) winds through the hills 16k/10m to the archaeological zone. Bear left at any fork in the road. The nicely-paved entrance road goes about 300 meters to the gate and parking area. There is a large map here which will help you get oriented. From here it is a short walk to the ruins (8–5 daily, Adm). There is a regular bus service from Poza Rica which goes past this area. Buses leave every hour and are marked "San Andrés" or "Agua Dulce."

El Tajín (el tah-heen') in Huastec means "place of smoke," and it was also a *Totonac* name for the rain god. Both groups inhabited the

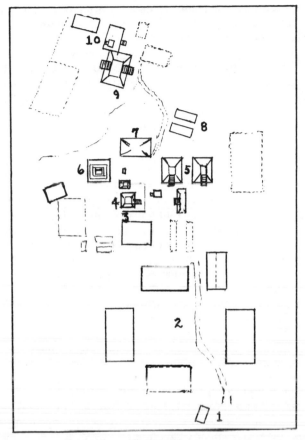

EL TAJIN

1. parking, entrance
2. path through plaza with stepped platforms
3. south ball court
4. multi-style pyramid
5. temple pyramids

6. pyramid of the niches
7. building A
8. north ball court
9. pseudo-niche pyramid
10. buildings for various civil functions

area. This fascinating site was discovered in 1785, and many archaeologists have worked there beginning with A. García Vega in 1935, but until recently much of what is known about the site was due to the work of J. García Payón from 1938 to 1962. In 1984 extensive excavation and restoration work was begun. It still continues under the archaeologist Héctor Cuevas. At least ten mounds have been uncovered, revealing different and intriguing structures. An on-site museum is also in the plans. **El Tajín** is destined to rival **Chichén-Itzá** and **Uxmal** as a primary site of archaeological importance and tourist attraction.

The first settlers were agricultural people with some arts and crafts, who built the first structures around 100–200 A.D. The first pyramid was built at this time. The area known as Tajín Chico (chee'-ko) was next constructed, between 300 and 400 A.D. From 500 to 600 there were certain **Teotihuacán** influences, and it was at this time that the famous Pyramid of the Niches (6)—365 of them—was built. The sides are 35 meters, and the 7 tiers are 25 meters high. The north ball court was also made during this period which brought much architectural activity and made Tajín the dominant culture from 650 to 800 A.D. Eventually, the center covered 9½ square kilometers, and the major structures 6,000 square meters (2,500 acres). Between 700 and 800 A.D. Monument (or building) "A" (10) with its eye-catching arched stairway was made, and some of the Tajín Chico complex.

About 900 A.D. the south ball court (3) with its exquisite sculptured panels was made. These portray the sacrifice of a ball player, the god of death, the adoration of the pulque plant, the god of lightning and thunder, personages in masks, and intertwined snakes. The symbols of sacrifice and death indicate the rise of a militaristic state. El Tajín, in fact, spread the sacrificial rites to the sun god and the famous "flying pole" performance associated with the eagle as a religious symbol. The stone for the ball courts (eventually there were seven of them) came from Río Cazones 35 k. away. The palace of columns (close to 4 ft. in diameter) on its 18 meter platform was constructed around 100 A.D. Certain *Toltec* influence infiltrated to el Tajín, but it was a Totonac center by this time. The city was abandoned some time between 1210 and 1230, possibly due to attacks or invasions by the *Otomí* or *Chichimec* groups, or even the neighboring Huastecs to the north. Dozens of mounds remain to be excavated. If you can, climb the hill overlooking the whole valley. A half-hidden path leads out from the section called Tajín Chico. You will get a magnificent view of the site and the valley.

You can return to highway 180 via Papantla from which you can also reach El Tajín (12k/8m). Papantla may be the vanilla capital of the world and you can buy extract or beans, some made into figures, at very reasonable prices. From here it is a fairly easy 208k/130m to Veracruz. The stretch just north of Nautla has the scenery that you see in travel brochures: tall, stately coconut palms with the sandy beach and the beautiful blue waters of the gulf in the background. 67k/41m south of Nautla you will pass Palma Sola. 10k/6m farther on a sign reads "Villa Rica" (not to be confused with "Playa Villa Rica," much closer to Palma Sola). A road to the left goes 1k to the seashore and the remains of the first Spanish settlement in Mexico. 3k farther south (and 74k/46.5m from Veracruz), right off the highway, you will see a large rock formation called Los Metates. On top of the hill in front of it is the unusual site of **Quiahuixtlán**. The Spaniards thought it was a fortress. Actually it was a walled city dating from 1200 B.C. complete with plazas, houses, temples, etc. But the unique feature is the cemetery made up of miniature temples about a meter high, complete with platforms and steps, set out in neat rows. But you will have to leave your car near the buildings along the highway and climb up the hill 20 meters (65 ft) to enjoy this rare spectacle. Buses ADO, AU or Teziutecos will take you from Jalapa to within walking distance of the site. These can be connected to from Veracruz at Cardel.

32k/20m farther on you will come to a road (right) with the sign **Cempoala** (sometimes "Z" is used instead of "C"). A blacktop road will take you 3k/1-1/4m to one of the gulf coast's most important archaeological sites: the *Iotonac* capital when the Spaniards first arrived in Mexico. The entrance is to your right, just as you reach the village (Mon-Sun, 8–6:00; Adm.). The site can also be reached from Veracruz (see 1-Bc below). ADO buses leave three times a day from Mexico City's east terminal for Cempoala.

Cempoala (sem-po-ah'-la) is probably a corruption of the Nahuatl name Cempohuallan, meaning "twenty waters." In colonial times, this site was known as Angostura. The first archaeological work was done in 1890 and the ruins were declared a national site in 1920. J. García Payón worked extensively in 1941. The site is mentioned in early Spanish chronicles because Cortés and his men landed not far from here, and this was the first large American city they saw. At the time, 1519, it had about 30,000 people and covered eight and a half square kilometers divided into walled precincts. The first constructions probably began around 800 A.D., although there is some evidence that Nahua refugees from **Teotihuacán**, which was destroyed in 650 A.D., settled there. The *Totonacs* eventually took it over and it became a major center and was probably known as Totonacapan.

The main walled area of the city, part of which is what the visitor sees today, covered 4,300 square meters. Still standing are some of the house platforms; the main temple, a rectangular structure of 13 tiers and remnants of the columns which supported the roof at the entrance; the 7-tiered pyramid of the "chimneys," so called because of the architectural design at the top; the temple to the wind god which combines rectangular and circular structures; the gladiatorial ring where hand-to-hand combats took place; the small circular structure for the "eternal fire"; and a short distance to the east, the temple of astronomy, or of the masks, which formerly had 52 clay masks symbolizing a cycle of years. Traces of the former yellow, red and blue colors can still be seen.

All of the above buildings were covered with white stucco, which must have shimmered in the tropical sun. A long platform structure on the west side was probably dedicated to the sun, and not far from it is a more recently uncovered pyramid in which some burials were found. Almost every conceivable artifact from stone points to effigy and polychrome pottery has been found at Cempoala. The small museum at the site contains some samples worth looking at.

Many of the mounds in the vicinity are still unexplored. There is one other pyramid you can visit, however. As you leave the site, turn right into the village and go two blocks, then turn left for a block. This semicircular structure is worth a brief visit.

16k/10m south from the Cempoala entrance at Cardel, there is a fine highway to Veracruz which is a great time saver. From Cardel Autotransportes Teziutecos leaves for Cempoala about every half hour. For things of archaeological interest in and near Veracruz see Route 1-B below.

1-B: DAYTRIPS IN THE VERACRUZ AREA

a) In the city itself, visit the museum located on Zaragoza street (west side) between Canal and Morales streets. This is about five blocks south of the main plaza and one block east. The *Totonac, Huastec* and *Olmec* pieces are particularly interesting. There is a fine sampling of the famous "smiling faces" of Remojadas, a good pottery collection, and some of the 782 jade pieces found in 1942 at **Cerro de las Mesas**, now closed to the public.

b) Jalapa (on Route 6-D) has an excellent museum which features the same cultures as the Veracruz museum. It is located on Av. Jalapa and 1o de Mayo. The round trip (238k/148m on highway 140) can be easily made in a day, or you can stay overnight in this capital of the state of Veracruz. There is regular bus service to Jalapa from Veracruz. Buses leave from the main terminal on Díaz Mirón street at the south end of town, and buses leave Mexico City's east terminal 32 times a day!

c) If you came to Veracruz by some other way than Route 1, you may want to visit **Cempoala**. Follow Zaragoza street north across the bridge, and the road to highway 180. 16k/10m past Cardel, the road to the ruins will be to your left. They are about 3k/1-1/4m from the highway. See the detailed description in Route 1-A. Driving time is a little over an hour. Buses going to cities north of Veracruz will take you as far as Cardel, and Autotransportes Teziutecos leaves from here for Cempoala every half hour.

d) The Isla de los Sacrificios (Isle of Sacrifices) lies about 8k/5m off shore. It was undoubtedly important in Pre-Columbian times, and there were some ruins of what was probably once a temple. The Spaniards who first came here found four mutilated humans, the victims of sacrifices— or so they assumed, since none of them had seen a sacrifice. Examples of pottery and statues that were found here are now in the Jalapa and Veracruz museums. There are small excursion boats to the island, now just a popular swimming spot.

e) For the very adventuresome, **Quiahuixtlán** is 74k/46.5m north of Veracruz. See Route 1-A for details. **Cempoala** ("c" above) can also be visited in the same daytrip.

1-C: VERACRUZ TO VILLAHERMOSA (478K/297M)

This route over highway 180 takes you through somewhat swampy country and into mountains with lush scenery. Most of the region you will travel through was once *Olmec* country.

One authority on Pre-Columbian Mexico calls these people the Tenocelome, "Those of the jaguar mouth." The first indications of this culture appeared along the gulf coast of Mexico, and this was long thought to be the center of both the origin and development of the Olmec culture. In recent years, archaeological finds are giving evidence that the Olmecs, or their ancestors, may have originated in the region of present-day eastern Guerrero and western Oaxaca, or a bit farther north where the Puebla, Morelos and Guerrero state borders meet. In any case, the formative stage of this culture began around 1500 B.C. with the unification of tribes or groups and the beginnings of cultural traits which may have included a ceramic tradition from the coast of Ecuador which spread north to Mexico. Around 1300 B.C. San Lorenzo (modern name) was established as one of the first permanent and important Olmec centers. The totemic concept of the were-jaguar seems to have developed during this time, represented as an infant man-jaguar, with a cleft or deformed human head with fangs. This representation may have sprung from one of the "origin legends" or myths. It is the reason for calling these people the Tenocelome.

By 800 B.C. the Olmecs had settled along the gulf coast and had established their main ceremonial center at **La Venta.** The feline motif appeared everywhere. Cultural traits included cranial deformation, dental mutilation, the rise of shamanism, and sculpture with fine, incised lines. There was some diffusion of the culture to the central highlands, and drawings representing celestial phenomena have been found at **Chalcatzingo** and **Juxtlahuaca**.

Between 800 and 200 B.C. the Olmec culture had its classic age.

Tres Zapotes was established (700 B.C.) and the Olmec influence spread as far as Nicaragua in the south and to western Mexico. This is evidenced by petroglyphs found in these areas, along with ceramic stamps and distinctive figurines, particularly the "baby-face" types with full cheeks and turned-down mouths, deformed heads, and no sex organs. This was a period of complex religious ceremonies, human sacrifices, the development of the calendar and astronomy, and above all megalithic sculpture, some of the monumental work weighing up to 200 tons. Oddly enough, stone structures were rather simple, and there was little use of mortar. Stelae were sculptured, mainly in a bas-relief form. Several of these, along with the well-known colossal heads, are displayed in Villahermosa Park. The stone for much of this sculpture came from the Tuxtla Gutiérrez mountains. The oldest known recorded New World date was found in 1939 by M. Stirling on a stela, but the corner of it was missing. A farmer plowed it out of his field thirty-four years later, and it was confirmed by Michael Coe of Yale University. The date is 31 B.C. The lower half of this stela is in the museum at **Tres Zapotes**.

The Olmec carried on an extensive trade, of which places like **Cerro de las Mesas** became focal points. They were adept at navigation by rafts, and had contacts with distant places—even as far as Florida. They were skilled jade workers and portable objects have been found at **Tlapacoya**, Tlatilco and even **El Opeño** near Lake Chalapa. The ball game, found throughout so much of Mexico, was played by the Olmecs, and may have been their invention. There is a strong similarity between Olmec art related to the game and the figures found at **Monte Albán** and **Dainzú**.

Disintegration of the Olmec culture probably came about through the invasion of other groups into their territory, particularly the Pipiles from Central America who simply absorbed them into their own migratory patterns or in some cases caused deliberate destruction. Remnants of the culture remained as part of later cultures, and the people, mixed with other groups, became the "historic Olmecs" whose most notable accomplishment was the taking of **Cholula** around 800 A.D.

The lower Gulf area is rich in archaeological sites. Unfortunately, the major *Olmec* sites like San Lorenzo, Macatapan, Totocapan, Tilapan, etc., are located in isolated areas where either there are no roads or there has been little development. The most important "finds" are now in museums, unhappily even outside of Mexico. U.S. institutions and archaeologists that have worked in the area have unscrupulously carted off many Mexican treasures. The U.S. Customs Service has recently seized and returned a number of stolen objects.

On the way south, you will drive through the Tuxtla Gutiérrez mountains and pass Lerdo de Tejada. There is a dirt road from here to **Tres Zapotes**, and a local bus service. A longer but better route a little farther on is via Santiago Tuxtla. If you go into the town (downhill to the right) you can see an excellent example of the huge Olmec heads. This one, in the plaza, is the largest ever found (40 tons). On one corner there is a small museum. A few Olmec sculptures are in the yard outside, and the museum itself contains samples of various Olmec arts. It is worth a brief visit (Tue-Sat. 9–6, Adm.; Sun, 9–3).

From Santiago it is possible to get to **Tres Zapotes**. Take the paved road from town toward Villa Isla until you reach Tibernal (21k/13m). A dirt road to the right goes straight to the town (20k/12.5m) and the museum (9–5, Adm.; Sun. free). The sculpture is astonishing, some of the best of its kind (*Olmec* art). Jaguars, serpents, enormous heads, stelae—it's all here.

24k/15m farther on you can visit scenic Lake Catemaco. In the middle of it is a large island which once had a Pre-Columbian center called **Agaltepeco**.

The ruins were described in 1925 by Franz Blom and Oscar LaFarge. J. Valenzuela carried out some excavations in 1945. This island city was occupied between 900 and 1000 A.D., perhaps as one of the centers of the "historic Olmecs," the roving *Toltec* groups or the *Totonacs*. The present mounds cover courts, plazas and walls. Much of the stone was used to build the houses of the present inhabitants of the island.

Farther along 180 at Acayucan trans-isthmus highway 185 begins. You can take it to join routes 6-B1 and 6-B2 rather than continue eastward. Continuing on 180, 40k/25m east of Coatzacoalcos a paved road goes some 8k/5m to **La Venta**.

La Venta (lah vein'-tah), possibly known as Tenocelome (tay-no-say-low'-may), was an important *Olmec* center which began around 1200 B.C. and flourished between 800 B.C. and 200 A.D. Originally the area was an island of three square kilometers which became an important ceremonial center. Because the Olmec culture had long been considered the oldest advanced culture in Mexico, this and other Olmec centers have been visited, investigated and excavated by many archaeologists. The universities of Tulane and California worked here in 1925 and 1955 respectively; M. Stirling (1940–42) and P. Drucker were here a number of times; M. Covarrubias made a map of the area in 1942; work was done by Coe, Berger, Graham and Heizer in 1967. From 1985 to 1988 excavation and restoration work was done on the 31-meter-high earth pyramid which was the central point of a line of plazas and structures running 750 meters in a north-south direction. The colossal stone heads, the altars, the stelae and the stone palisade have all been moved to a park in Villahermosa, but there is a museum at the site itself (daily, 8–5). This site spread its influence as far as El Salvador in the south, western Mexico, the whole gulf coast of Mexico and even to Florida which had contact with the site around 400 A.D. The Olmecs themselves may have been forced out by groups moving from **Chiapa del Corzo** or the Petén area to the south. The important finds here include the oldest calendar date in glyph form, eleven colossal heads of basalt stone and three dedicatory offerings in the form of mosaic masks of semi-precious stone (one of 486 pieces) which were deliberately buried after having been made. Villahermosa park has a reproduction of one of these, and of the whole La Venta layout.

Continuing east on 180, you will come to Cárdenas. Here, a paved road to the left will take you to **Comalcalco** about 38k/23m north. Go 2 miles beyond the town itself. Signs indicate the road (r) to the archaeological area is not far from the highway. Work has been going on at this site off and on for many years, and it is almost a must for anyone traveling in this part of Mexico (10–4, Adm). ADO buses to Comalcalco leave twice a day from Mexico City's east terminal, and "Servico Somellera" leaves from Villahermosa's second class bus station every 30 minutes.

Comalcalco (ko-mahl-kahl'-ko) means "the house of the earthenware griddle." This fascinating site was visited and explored in 1856 and 1888, but it was Franz Blom who did the first archaeological work in 1925. G. Ekholm worked there in 1956, and excavations and restoration have been going on since 1971. Comalcalco is the westernmost *Maya* site, and may have been the capital of the Chontalpe region. One legend says it was the city of the Maya prince Tabscoob (hence, the name Tabasco). The architecture is of the classic Maya style, like that found farther south at **Palenque**, but fired brick was used for the masonry, and this site is the only instance of such usage. A few of the standing ruins show the typical corbelled arches. Lime and oyster shells were used to make the cement. There are some twelve mounds in the area, in two main groups. The first constructions here are on the north side. They have adobe centers and are covered with bricks, often stuccoed over. What is now known as Temple Palace I is in this area. The walls had painted Maya figures, and there was a subterranean tomb. Temple IV had glyphs, masks, seated personages and a serpent head as decorations. The second group, to the south, was the palace, consisting of two long corridors with rooms. Several elaborate tombs have been found in the area, also. No polychrome pottery and no dated inscriptions have been found. A good portion of the north group has been restored and is well worth visiting. Materials found during the excavations are in a museum at the site.

Returning to highway 180 via Jalpa will save you 37k/23m. Villahermosa has two fine archaeological attractions. The La Venta Park (8–4:30, Adm) is located on the right side of highway 180, a short distance past the road into the airport. There is a small museum at the entrance. The setting enhances the feeling of actually experiencing the past. A mile south of town, on the river front, is the Research Center of *Olmec* and *Mayan* Cultures. This multi-storied building houses what can probably be considered Mexico's second best museum (Tue-Sun, 9–8; Adm), though Jalapans might disagree! City bus No. 1 or those marked "CICOM" pass by here. From La Venta park, return to the clock circle and take Paseo Tabasco all the way to the river front drive (Malecón) and turn right.

From Villahermosa it is possible to fly in light aircraft to **Bonampak**, **Yaxchilán** and **Palenque**, though the last mentioned site is easily accessible by road (see Route 2-B). This city is also the starting point for highway 195 south which joins the Pan American highway (Route 6-C) to the Guatemala border, or back into central Mexico.

Route 2: The Yucatán Peninsula

Villahermosa, in the heart of the state of Tabasco, is not the Yucatán peninsula, but it is the best starting place for the routes which lead there. It is possible to fly or go by bus to Mérida and work out from there with tour groups, in buses or in a rented car (around $300 a week for the simplest kind, plus the extra cost per kilometer).

Politically, the peninsula is divided into three states: Campeche, Yucatán and Quintana Roo.

Campeche was the *Maya* province of Ah-Kin-Pech and is the westernmost portion of the peninsula along the Gulf of Mexico. There are 254 recognized archaeological sites in the state. Seven are considered pre-classic, and include **Dzibilnocac**. The rest of the sites are either classic or post-classic, and many have been grouped according to architectural style (some indications of their characteristics will be given at specific sites): 26 in the Petén style, 123 Río Bec, 15 Chene, 35 Puuc, 10 T-Cheh' and 14 Mayapán. Southern Campeche is heavily forested and many of the sites are literally lost in the jungle. It was in the coastal town of Champotón that Cortés was given the Indian girl who became known as Doña Marina or "La Malinche," and who accompanied him throughout the conquest, proving invaluable as an interpreter for the Spaniards. The *Maya* sites in this state which can be visited are indicated in the text of Routes 2-A and 2-F.

Quintana Roo is named after a poet associated with the independence movement, Andrés Quintana Roo. Geographically it comprises the eastern part of the Yucatán peninsula along the Caribbean and is divided into three zones: the Petén in the south (which continues into Guatemala), the Río Bec area and the coast. Innumerable *Maya* sites are located in this territory; 71 have been identified as follows: 2 pre-classic, 10 classic, 24 late classic and 35 post-classic. In addition, there are 25 known but unstudied coastal sites. In 1989 an archaeological investigating team under R. MacNeish visited 108 sites in the state and found surface remains in 84 of them. Because of the dense rainfall and tropical foliage in the southern part of the state, very few of the archaeological sites are easily accessible. The highway along the coast has helped open up some of them.

Between these two states, in a kind of V wedge, lies the state of Yucatán. It is basically arid and filled with dense scrub forest. The whole peninsula is something like a huge block of limestone. The underground passages and porous surface provided the famous "cenotes" or wells which were the source of water and sometimes the site of sacrifices for the Pre-Columbian people. Most of this region is gently rolling country and there is no difficult driving. Archaeologically it is undoubtedly the most fascinating in Mexico.

It was to these present-day states that the Maya Culture spread and developed from both the south and the west. The Ministry of Tourism is currently working with the governments of Belize, Guatemala, Honduras and El Salvador to set up a **Maya Route** which will take the tourist to sites in these countries on a "circle route." Here we should say something about these highly talented and still somewhat mysterious people.

Like the *Chichimecs, Maya* is a name given to several groups of people who spoke the same language. They lived on the Yucatán peninsula and in the present-day states of Tabasco and Chiapas in Mexico, in Guatemala, and in parts of Honduras and El Salvador. The formative stage of the culture has traditionally been set around 1500 B.C. but recent excavations show that it may have been even earlier when groups living in various parts of the above-mentioned regions began to live together and communicate through trade. **Dzibil-chaltún** was one of these centers. From 1150 to 400 B.C. the pottery style and cultural traits of the Mamón group were predominant. They were replaced by the Chicanel for about two centuries, and then the Matzanel influence took over. During this time a numbering system began, along with the calendar. Ceramics had animal forms for supports; zoomorphic altars were made.

The Tzakol influence from 250 to 600 A.D. brought about the classic period of Maya culture. It had three special characteristics: poly-chrome pottery, carved stelae with dates and inscriptions and stone temples using the corbel (or vaulted) arch. These traits were brought by groups from the Pacific coast of Guatemala who moved to the highlands and to the Petén area. The oldest inscribed stela of this period is from 292 A.D. During this period the Putún group moved to the **Chichén-Itzá** area, and then to Champotón on the coast.

Between 600 and 900, Tepeu-style pottery was widespread. Stepped pyramid platforms, altars and temples abounded because the priestly class was governing. Astronomy became an important science and observatories were built. The ball game was played everywhere, usually three against three, though sometimes the teams got as large as eight on a side. Architecture was done in the Puuc style which was characterized by a) stone sculpture which was assembled into designs, masks, etc. to form a "mosaic veneer" on the façade of buildings, and b) rows of short columns used as a decorative element. This is best seen at sites like **Kabah**, **Labná**, **Sayil** or even **Edzná**. In Chiapas, **Palenque** became the great center, while others like **Yaxchilán** and Piedras Negras developed. In southern Yucatán a different style of architecture developed in the Río Bec area and spread northward to **Xpujil**, **Dzibilnocac** and other centers. On the Caribbean coast, the port city of **Tulum** was thriving, along with other cities in that region like **Cobá**. Eventually there were 12 political divisions on the peninsula.

Then, slowly but surely, the civilization declined. Scholars still debate the causes and reasons—the "why?" of such a strange occurrence. There is growing evidence that the downfall came as a result of widespread internal revolution, the rise of the masses against the exacting and domineering priest-rulers.

Around the middle of the tenth century, Maya groups from Tabasco and Campeche, mixed with migrating *Toltec* groups, began a Maya renaissance, first at **Chichén-Itzá** and then at **Uxmal** and **Mayapán**. These cities formed a League and for a time the culture and civilization prospered again. Internal dissensions grew, however, and an all-out war brought the downfall of Mayapán in 1441. Uxmal and Chichén-Itzá lasted only a while longer. The Itzá people moved south to the Petén region and established a new city at Tayasal. The Spaniards did not completely subdue it until 1697. Descendents of the Maya lived in Quintana Roo and Yucatán and in the terrible "War of the Castes" in 1901, according to some statistics, 300,000 of them were killed. Today, remnants of the Maya people live in the secluded jungle areas of Chiapas, and are known as Lacandones.

The Maya were obsessed with time and the recording of things in a chronological framework. There were eighteen months of twenty days, and a five-day period which belonged to no month. All of the Maya glyphs relating to time have been deciphered, and everything begins from August 11, 3114 B.C. (according to Thompson; October 14, 3373 according to Spinden). There are about 1000 known glyphs, of which perhaps 40% have been deciphered already. D. Kelly, L. Schele and D. Stuart have added much in recent years. Maya art and architecture were extraordinary. In building, limestone cement was used (which is why many of the ruins still stand) along with hardwoods for doorframes, ceiling beams, etc. Later structures strongly resemble *Toltec* architecture, an influence which it definitely did experience. In the minor arts, the Maya craftsmen excelled in working jadite, serpentine, coral and gold. The sculptured stelae are unsurpassed anywhere in the Americas and represent baroque art long before Europe had it. Now, let's take a look at these places.

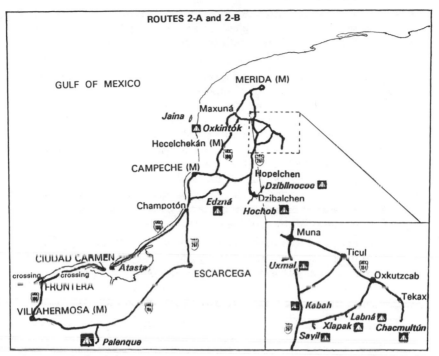

ROUTES 2-A and 2-B

GULF OF MEXICO

MERIDA (M)

Jaina ◊   Maxuná
         ▲ *Oxkintók*
Hecelchekán (M)

CAMPECHE (M)   Hopelchen
                ▲*Dziblinocoo* ▲
Champotón   *Edzná* ▲   ~Dzibalchen
                    Hochob ▲

Muna

CIUDAD CARMEN   *Atasta*
crossing   crossing   ESCARCEGA   *Uxmal* ▲   Ticul   Oxkutzcab
FRONTERA
VILLAHERMOSA (M)   Tekax
                    ▲ *Kabah*
▲ *Palenque*   *Labná* ▲
                Xlapak ▲   *Chacmultún* ▲
                Sayil ▲

2-A: VILLAHERMOSA TO MÉRIDA VIA HIGHWAY 180 (571K/356M)

The traveler on highway 180 should be forewarned that there are four ferry boat crossings which can delay the trip sometimes even several hours. The 125k/78m saved by taking this route can easily be lost time-wise. 168k/105m and three ferry boat crossings from Villahermosa, you enter the city of Ciudad Carmen. There is a small museum here. It is located near the end of the road to Playa Norte. This road, which goes south from the ferry boat landing, is on the west side of the main plaza. The museum has artifacts from the nearby burial sites of Ciurelos and **Atasta**.

The site was studied by Matthew Stirling in 1957. Only late post-classic pottery has been found (1300–1500 A.D.). A standing figure is perhaps *Toltec* in origin. Most of the knowledge of the site has come from burials and there are no important standing structures.

After one more ferry boat crossing, it is a fairly easy drive to Campeche. At Champotón you can take a circle route to Campeche and visit **Edzná** (see Route 2-B). In Campeche one museum (Tue-Sun, 8–5) is located in an old fort on the gulf front called Baluarte de la Soledad and has a number of *Mayan* stelae. A more complete and attractive collection is in the Regional Museum on calle 59, between calles 14 and 16 (Tue-Sat, 9–2, 5–8; Sun, 9–1). It is notable especially for its collection of **Jaina** figurines.

Jaina (high'-nah) is an island located off the western shore of the Yucatán peninsula, north of Campeche. This seems to have been primarily a burial site, and some 225 graves have been found. H. Modeano worked here in 1946, and R. Piña Chan in 1948. There are two major areas: Sacpol and Sayssala, containing some ruined structures, one forty feet tall. The most notable discoveries have been the figurines in great number and variety, both hand modeled and mold-made, high ornate, realistic and imaginative, and some of the "fine orange" ceramics. There are examples in the museum in Campeche and in several other museums. The island has been closed to visitors because of the constant grave-looting.

At Chencoyí, highway 180 turns north for Mérida. This whole area is full of old *Maya* towns and ruins, few readily accessible. 71k/43m from Campeche in Hecelchakan there is a museum of several rooms of fine pieces from nearby **Jaina** and a large model of a *Mayan* town. It is located on the north side of the plaza (Tue-Sat, 9–5, Adm) on the main road. A stela stands in front of it.

For the next site, after you by-pass Maxcanú and just beyond the railroad tracks a narrow paved road (r) goes 11k/7m to Calcehtok. From here it is 4k up a dirt road south to **Oxkintok**. If you can handle the Spanish, in Calcehtok ask for Roger (but say row'-hair), father or son. Both are expert guides to the site.

This site was studied by E. M. Shook in 1940. The ruins may cover more than nine square kilometers. There are three sectors: Dzib, Ah-Canul and May. Excavations were done from 1986–1989 on the last two groups. The large pyramid is in the May group. In between the May and Dzib groups is a single edifice called "Satunsat" (Labyrinth). It seems to have been used for religious ceremonies. The Ah Canul group had 5 plazas with some 20 structures. There are remains of several pyramids, most of them in rather deteriorated condition. From 215 to 474 A.D. there was intense architectural activity here, and several different styles are evident, one clearly related to northern Guatemala, and another to the Puuc style. 26 stelae, some of them paneled, have been found, and the figures seem to be different from the Maya type usually represented. This has been interpreted as a change of ethnic composition in the late period of Maya history. This site may have been the center of a "state" which extended to **Dzibilchaltún** on the north and **Edzná** on the south. The city was abandoned around the tenth century.

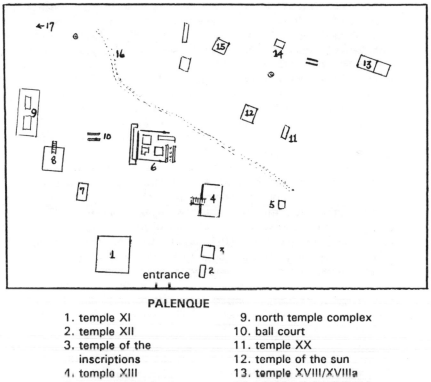

PALENQUE

1. temple XI
2. temple XII
3. temple of the inscriptions
4. temple XIII
5. house of the jaguar
6. palace complex/tower
7. temple X
8. temple of the Count
9. north temple complex
10. ball court
11. temple XX
12. temple of the sun
13. temple XVIII/XVIIIa
14. temple of the foliated cross
15. temple of the cross
16. river channel
17. to the museum

The Calcehtok road continues east to Muna where you can join Route 2-B. For sites in and around Mérida see Route 2-C.

2-B: VILLAHERMOSA TO MÉRIDA VIA HIGHWAYS 186 AND 261 (696K/434M)

From Villahermosa it is 114k/71m east on highway 186 to the road (right) which goes to **Palenque**. A drive of 27k/17m brings you to a fork in the road. The left branch goes into town; the right one goes to the archaeological zone, one of the most beautiful in Mexico. There are buses (ADO) several times a day from Villahermosa, once a day from Mérida, and twice a day from Mexico City (east terminal) to the town of Palenque (also called Santo Domingo). A regular van service to the ruins leaves from Hidalgo & Allende.

Palenque (pah-len'-kay: daily, 8–5; Adm. except Sun) means "palisade." For a long time the site was known as Nachan. This city was one of the great *Maya* centers and originally covered an area from 24 to 32 square kilometers. In the seventh century A.D. it was the **Teotihuacán** of the east.

Stelae found here, and other inscriptions, have revealed part of the fascinating history of the center. From 583 to 604 A.D. it was ruled by a woman, Kan Ik, and again from 612–615 by Zac Kuk. Then came Pacal who had a long and apparently great reign from 615 to 683. In the following year his son Chan Bahlum took over. The city collapsed some time around 810 A.D. The last known date, carved on a vessel, is 799. This history and other archaeological facts were discoveries resulting from the work of many archaeologists over the years. The site was known to the Spaniards, and J. L. Stephens wrote about it in the 1840's; the first serious investigations began in 1923 by F. Blom, and complemented by the work of M. Fernández (1934), A. Ruz (1945–1952), C. Sáenz (1954) and I. Marquina (1957), among others. The general characteristics of Palenque are: stepped platforms, double-chambered rooms, the false arch, roof combs, and decorations with hieroglyphs and modeled or carved human figures. These latter have deformed heads, almond eyes, thin lips, a long "roman" nose with no break in the bridge, highly ornate headdresses, and a good amount of jewelry. All of the sculpture work here is highly artistic, almost exquisite.

There are two important buildings in the central complex. The Temple of the Inscriptions is where in 1952 Ruz found the magnificent sarcophogus of Pacal (3). The stairway leading down to the burial spot under the pyramid (almost 90 ft.) took four years to clear out (open 10–4). The beautifully sculptured lid weighs five tons. The walls on the temple on top are filled with carved hieroglyphics (620!) which relate Pacal's history.

The Palace (6) covers an area of 70 × 55 meters. The four-story tower is unique in Maya architecture, and many believe it was an observatory. Near the south complex of four small temples is a burial crypt for victims sacrificed at funeral rites. The ball court and other temples are in the north complex. The museum here is open 10–5.

There is a dirt road from Palenque to **Bonampak**, but it is passable only in dry weather, and then only in a jeep. The trip should not be made without a guide, especially if there is interest in trying to visit some of the other ruins hidden away in the jungle, like **Yaxchilán**. These sites are only for those who are willing to rough it. There are organized trips from Palenque (agencies on Juárez and Allende streets) but they are expensive and require a lot of rugged living. (Both sites open 8–4, Adm.)

Bonampak (bone-ahm-pock') is located deep in the Chiapas jungle. The name means "painted walls" and was given by Sylvanus Morley. It was discovered in 1946 by Giles Healy, a photographer, and Carl Fry. It has been studied by experts such as K. Ruppert, J. Eric Thompson and Tatiana Proskouriakoff (1955). Situated in the Lacanjá river valley, the site until recently was reached by plane to Agua Azul and a three-day trip with pack animals. The site itself existed by 600 A.D. and consisted mainly of small buildings, such as the three-room temple (S1) where the famous paintings were made. These were done in fresco fashion, in about 48 hours, somewhere around 800 A.D., shortly before the collapse of the city. They are marvellous for detail and realism, and exalt the human figure. The first scene is the presentation to the nobles of the heir-apparent of Bonampak, and is enlivened by dancing figures and musicians. The second room portrays a battle with a neighboring group and takes place in a forest. The judgment and punishment of the prisoners is also depicted, but of even greater interest are the details of dress, such as the jaguar skin sandals, helmets, etc. The third scene portrays the victory feast, the nobles watching dancers and acrobats and listening to musicians. Through the vivid colors and the realistic portrayal, the whole *Maya* world comes alive. The famous paintings are almost faded out now, but perfect copies of them done by Rina Lazo exist in the museum in Mexico City. There are remains of several other buildings of different architectural styles, witnessing to the evolution of the city and its role as a contact point between the north and south Mayan groups. Some stelae were also found at the site, one of them nearly 16 feet tall and 9 feet wide (5×3 meters) which depicts Hatach Huinic, the king who defeated the *Olmecs*.

Despite the fact that **Yaxchilán** (yahsh-chee-lahn'—the name means "green stones") is lost in the Chiapas jungle on the Usumacinta river, it has been frequently visited. The site is reached in the same way as **Bonampak**, except that river transport is used, and even that is difficult to get to. Both Maudsley and Charney were here in 1882. Maler visited in 1885, 1897 and 1900; Ruppert in 1931; and Satterthwaite in 1934. Tulane University archaeologists investigated here in 1940, and T. Proskouriakoff worked here in 1960–64. R. Pavón reconstructed the 7-tiered Temple 3 in 1963. Excavations have also been made by R. García Moll and continue sporadically. There are many identified but unexcavated buildings. One of these, called Building 21, was excavated in 1983. Four of the temples at this classic *Maya* site were built between 692 and 726 A.D. The lintels are of worked stone, often with hieroglyphs. The roofs have "combs" (small narrow walls) of the "dovecote" (like lattice work) variety, but with smooth surfaces. Numerous stelae have been found, with 125 inscriptions. From them, and from the art which has conflict and warriors as its subject, it has been learned that around 701 Shield Jaguar, possibly a usurper from Guatemala, took over the rule and consolidated it through marriage alliances (three known wives) and territorial expansion. Bird Jaguar who ruled from 752 to 770 continued the tradition of warfare and conquest, and many of the buildings still standing were constructed during his reign. The last stela dates are between 810 and 840. After that this site like so many others at the same time was abandoned.

Return to highway 186 which continues to Escárcega and straight across the peninsula to Chetumal (Route 2-F). ADO has several departures daily for both of these cities from the east terminal in Mexico City. From Escárcega highway 261 goes north and merges with highway 180 at Champotón. 14k/9m farther northeast highway 188 (right) will take you 60k/37m to **Edzná** (daily, 8–5; Adm.) There is one bus a day from Campeche, but there is guaranteed round trip transportation with the morning guided tour of "Viajes Programados" (Calle 59 & coastal highway; very reasonable).

Edzná (ed-sna') means "house of echoes." The site was reported in 1927 by N. Quinta. E. Palacios worked here in 1936, and A. Ruz between 1943 and 1945. Excavations began in 1958 (A. Ruz, R. Pavón, C. Sáenz) and were continued from 1970–72 and 75–76 by R. Piñaq Chan. In 1986–87 Luis Millet headed further excavations, and in 1989 William Follan and Antonio Benevides began working here behind the palace where several large stucco masks have been discovered. Although it is known mainly as a classic Maya site, the area had been inhabited as early as 600 B.C. Most of the dates found on stelae and monuments range from 550 to 810 A.D. There is a strong possibility that the rulers here were related to the Sky Dynasty at Tikal (Guatemala).

While the architecture follows the Puuc tradition, a somewhat individualistic and "non-conformist" style also developed, and is evident in the major structures. The whole archeological zone covers more than three square kilometers and has been mapped by archaeologists from the New World Foundation and Brigham Young University, but it is the main plaza which is of greatest interest. This huge area (170 meters) is flanked on one side by a platform 6 meters high, and almost as long as the plaza itself. On this stands a five-tiered building (Nohol Na) erected in 650 A.D. with a massive, almost monolithic stairway up the center to the top level, and rooms on each of the five levels. On top is one of the "roof combs" 6 meters high, with masks and stucco serpents and jaguar heads. The pyramid structure to the north was possibly a priest's quarters. Ruins also include the Temple of the Stelae, the Temple of the Old Woman, and the walls of a ball court on which excavations have begun. Two of the stelae from here are in the Campeche museum.

41k/26m east from where the Edzná road joins highway 201 you will see some ruins right on the highway, to the left. There isn't a whole lot to see, but you will get a very good idea of why archaeologists have such a problem in this area, and how ruins can disappear so easily under vegetation. This was probably Toheok. Today it is called **Hopelchén**. The site was partially excavated by Tulane University in 1940 and by I. Marquina in 1950. Little is known about it except that it was a late classic site (600–900 A.D.) where the Chenes style of architecture seems to have been predominant. For the very adventuresome, there are two "lost in the jungle" and intriguing sites which can be reached from here, but don't attempt them during the wet season! A road (269) south from Hopelchén goes to Dzibalchén. Before you reach the town a sign (right) indicates the way to Chencoh (9k/5m). When you get there, take a left at the second road and go about a block. Make another left and you are on a really rustic road which goes 4k/2-1/2m into the jungle. When the road branches, turn left and the ruins of **Hochob** are visible on the hill. Many of the former buildings are much crumbled, but if any site offers a good idea of the challenges archaeologists face, this one certainly does. There is enough still in good condition to make the trip worthwhile.

Hochob was visited by T. Maler in 1887, and E. Seler published a site plan and photographs in 1916. R. Robina studied the area and described it in 1956, and G. F. Andrews was here in 1974, 1978 and 1983. Reconstruction work was done in 1982–1983 under the direction of R. Carrasco on Structures 1, 2, 5 and 6. The last two are temple buildings. The general architecture is an outstanding example of the Chenes style and has many similarities to **Chicanná**, especially the splendid example of Maya baroque with the whole facade of the main building forming one huge monster mask. The lattice-work decoration at the end columns is a unique touch.

Back on the road, continue to Dzibalchén and from here on a paved road northeast to Vicente Guerrero. A dirt road out from the main plaza goes into the forest where the first road to the right will take you to the ruins of **Dzibilnocac** (62k/40m from the highway; Mon-Sun, 8–5). There are several buses a day which make the 3-hour trip from Campeche to Dzibalchén. Local buses go to V. Guerrero.

Dzibilnocac (zee-bill-no-cock') was visited by E. Seler in 1916 and by H. Pollock in 1936 and 1949. Nelson and R. Carrasco did some work here in the mid-70's. Pottery found here shows that the site was occupied from 500 B.C. to 1000 A.D. There are remains of three temple pyramids. The main attraction is a structure (A-1) of three towers. This underwent restoration in 1982–83. The central one supports an imitation temple, similar to the Río Bec style. One tower has a two-room chamber on top with stairs on either side of the tower. Most of the material found here is in the Mérida museum.

At Hopelchén, the highway turns north. One mile after you pass the stone arch which marks the boundry between Campeche and Yucatán you will come to a new road (31–right) which takes you to the sites of **Sayil**, **Xlapak** and **Labná**, and the Loltún cave.

Sayil (sah-yeel': 8–5; Adm.) dates from the late classic Maya period, around 850 A.D. It was investigated by E. M. Shook in 1940, and T. Proskouriakoff in 1950. Only a few of the buildings have been rescued from the surrounding jungle. The Palace, built on three levels, contains 100 rooms. The decorative columns are typical of the Puuc style. This building is less ornate than those of **Labná** and **Kabah**. Somewhat unique features are the rectangular niches over the doors on the third level, and the fact that the first level is built in two different styles. The second floor has a representation of the bee god, Ah Muzen-Cab, patron of merchants. The building known as the Mirador (Lookout) was actually a temple pyramid. The ball court indicates that this was a rather important center. Pottery from here has been styled "regional polychrome," which means that it has certain local and distinctive features. Some statues are still scattered about in the forest. A path from the Mirador will take you to the Stela of the Phallus.

Xlapak (shla-pock': 8–5) is 5k/3.5m from Sayil. The palace (20 meters long) built in the Puuc style is the most important structure. The different architectural styles here indicate an evolution in Maya art. The frieze work which runs the length of the building is a remarkable mosaic in stone work. The masks on the corners represent Chac, the rain god.

3.5k from the preceding site you come to **Labná** (Lahb-nah': 8–5, Adm. except Sun) which means "old ruined buildings" and was probably given to the site by E. H. Thompson who visited it in 1892. Like **Kabah** and **Sayil**, this is an early Maya site where the Puuc style, characterized by the elaborate decorative mosaic stone work and the use of the short "columns" as ornamentation has some of its best representation. There are three striking structures here. The pyramid is 15 meters high, and has a "roof comb" over 10 meters tall. The palace shows evidence of three phases of construction. The façade (90 meters) is entirely decorated, but in three different styles. The splendid archway marked the road to **Kabah**.

The road you have been taking passes the Loltún cave (28k/18m from **Labná**) and ends at Oxkutzcab on highway 184 which you can take back to 261. Opinions differ about the Loltún cave which you could also visit. It was certainly known and used by the Maya people, but it has nothing spectacular to offer archaeologically speaking. You can make much better use of your time at ruins still to come before you reach Mérida. If you want an interesting side trip, at Oxkutzcab turn east 18k/11m toward Tekax. Just before reaching the town a paved road south past Cancab leads to **Chacmultún**.

This large center, "the hill of red rock," covers about one square kilometer and has three groups of buildings: a) straight ahead from where you leave your car you will find the Chacmultún group with three palaces on platforms, the main one with 16 rooms, and 2-meter columns at the entrance. The west side is highly decorated. The other two buildings are in poor condition but there are some benches, altars and remnants of paintings. b) The Xeth Pool area, reached by a dirt road going south from where you parked, has some platform bases and a lot of rooms in one color (red) with representations of snakes. c) The Cabal Pak group, farther on and up a hill, has buildings juxtapositioned on a natural hill to look like one huge edifice. This center was at its height around 800 A.D., but probably dates from pre-classic times.

You can return to highway 184 and take it to either Ticul or Muna. At Ticul, you can turn back toward highway 261 and reach it just a bit north of the ruins of **Kabah**, or you can take 184 to Muna and turn south. The ruins lie on both sides of the highway, but the most important buildings are on the east side.

Kabah (kah-bah'—8–5, Adm. except Sun), situated in a fertile valley with hills for defense, is one of several early sites studied by A. Ruz in 1948. The most notable structure is the elaborately ornate "Palace of the Masks" with the whole façade covered with inlaid stone work arranged to represent continuous feline faces or "monster masks" said to represent Chac, the rain god. The building is 47 meters long and has 10 inner chambers. To the north of this building is the Teocalli, 25 meters high. The Temple of the Lintels has red painted hands inside, the symbol of Itzamná (see **Izamal**). There are six other structures including a Phallic Temple. The beautiful arch marks the beginning of the causeway or road to **Labná** and **Uxmal**. The architecture here is in the Puuc style. The pottery found is a regional polychrome, and burials were made in funeral chambers. The main palace is sometimes referred to as the Codz Po'op or "rolled up straw mat," a reference, perhaps, to the columns. A

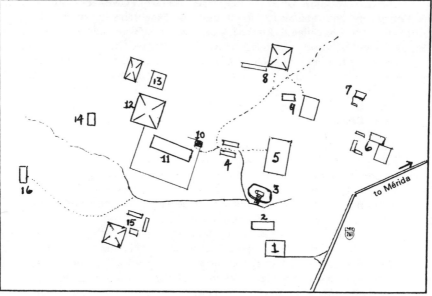

UXMAL

I. parking	9. columns group
2. tourist center	10. house of the turtles
3. house of the magician	11. governor's palace
4. ball court	12. great pyramid
5. the "nunnery"	13. house of the doves
6. north quadrangle	14. Chimez temple
7. northwest group	15. house of the old woman
8. cemetery	16. phallic temple

Spanish archaeological team is doing reconstruction work behind the great palace.

There is no public bus directly to this site. Some long-distance buses to Campeche do go past Kabah. They leave from the main bus terminal in Mérida. These same buses also pass **Uxmal** (below). There are organized tours from Mérida (96k/60m). You can easily do this by car also if you do not have time to visit all of the sites, and there is still one more!

22k/14m north of Kabah is the site of **Uxmal**, one of the great Maya cities.

Uxmal (oosh-mahl'—8–5; Adm. except Sun; "light and sound" show in English at 9 p.m. daily) is a sort of awesome place. The name is probably more correct as Oxmal, or "built three times." Long known (J. L. Stephens was here in 1841), excavations were undertaken in 1936 and 1938, and reconstruction was done under the supervision of J. A. Erosa. This site has been visited and investigated by many archaeologists. Considerable restoration took place between 1970–1974, and work is currently going on in back of the Governor's Palace. The first structures were built in styles found at **Hochob**, **Dzibilnocac** and **Río Bec** between 987 and 1007 A.D. Around 1194, Uxmal formed an alliance with **Mayapán** and **Chichén-Itzá**. Dissentions plagued the League of Mayapán and at one point Uxmal was attacked by men from that city. Successfully defended, Uxmal in turn became belligerent and in 1441 attacked and partially destroyed Mayapán. Uxmal itself was abandoned shortly afterwards.

Some facts about the various structures (numbers refer to the map of Uxmal): the so-called House of the Magician or Sorcerer (3) is really five superimposed pyramids. The most unusual feature is the elliptical base. The total structure is 31.5 meters tall, and the temple on top is 22 × 3.9 meters. As late as 1656, offerings of copal and coca were found before idols in the inner chambers. The "nunnery" (5), so called because it reminded the Spaniards of a cloister, may in fact have been a residence of virgins in charge of the sacred fire. The courtyard is 78 × 65 meters. The surrounding buildings contain 88 rooms. Many of the lintels in these buildings are of the original wood, which is from the sapodilla tree. The Governor's House (11) rests on an enormous base 151 × 178 × 11 meters. The house itself is 97 meters long. The Adoratory behind it was excavated between 1951–1952 by C. Sáenz and A. Ruz. A jade necklace found here is in the museum in Mérida. The House of the Turtles (10) is 28 × 10 × 6 meters. The ball court (4) is 34 × 21 meters; the rings are 1.1 meters in diameter. The House of the Doves (13) is so called because the "roof comb" openings give the appearance of a dovecote. It is 72 meters long. This may be the oldest building at Uxmal. The House of the Old Woman (15), a very deteriorated structure is so called because a mutilated 1.30 meter statue of a woman was found a short distance from the pyramid base. About 400 meters south of the previous structure there is a Phallic Temple (16). The rain spouts, one of which remains, were in the shape of phalli. Uxmal was joined by a causeway to **Kabah** 22k/14m to the southeast.

If it is getting late and you fear you may not make it to Mérida (and you don't want to be driving at night!) you can find lodging in either Muna or Ticul, not far away. This would also give you the opportunity to come back and see more the next day. There is also a three or four-star hotel right at Uxmal itself, and new motels have sprung up along highway 261.

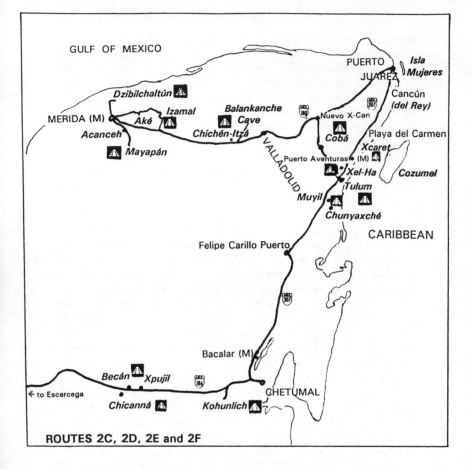

ROUTES 2C, 2D, 2E and 2F

2-C: DAYTRIPS OUT FROM MÉRIDA

If you have taken Route 2-A to Mérida and missed all of the sites along 2-B, or have taken the bus from Mexico City (ADO has 8 departures daily from the east terminal) or have flown directly to Mérida from the States, it is possible to visit many Mayan centers within a day's trip from Mérida, and even several on the same day. If you don't want to go on your own, there are several agencies in Mérida which offer organized trips. There are Tourist Office booths in the airport and the bus station, and a main office on Calle 60 at the corner with Calle 57.

C1: To the north, there is the fascinating center of **Dzibilchaltún**, 27k/17m away. Take highway 261 north toward Progreso. 23k/15m from Mérida you will see a road to the right which goes (7k/4m) into a town. Signs indicate the way to the archaeological area. This is a somewhat popular place with the local residents, because the cenote is now used as a public swimming pool. There is bus service from Mérida to Progreso. The station is on Calle 62, between Calles 65 and 67. It is 4k from the highway to the ruins.

Dzibilchaltún (zee-beel-chahl-toon': 8–5, Adm. except Sun) means "written on flat stone". This is one of the oldest continuous settlements in the New World. It has been occupied since 2000 B.C. Between 800 and 200 B.C. it became a major settlement, and people lived in an area estimated at 80 square kilometers, 16 of which were densely populated and constructed. The florescent period was from 900 to 1100 A.D. In 1963–64, 31 square kilometers were mapped and showed 8,526 structures. There were probably about 20,000 altogether. Architecture varies from mud walls to stone masonry. The ceremonial construction was done during the later periods. In the 1940's and again from 1956–1961 E. W. Andrews worked here, and it is to his work that we owe much of our knowledge of this site. The most widely known structure is the Temple of the Seven Dolls, so called because of the figurines found there. It was built in 183 A.D. The platform which supports the temple has stairways on all four sides—a feature found later at **Chichén-Itzá**. One structure (No. 450) is the last of three superimposed, showing that this practice also existed at an early date. There are remains of a causeway 2.40 meters high, 18 meters wide and almost two and a half k. long. Remains of the corbelled arch and a skull rack show the late *Maya* influence. Many of the later buildings used materials from earlier constructions, and also fragments of stelae. This happened during the decandent period when **Mayapán** was a dominant power. Nearby there is the large Xlacah cenote, or sacrificial well. It is 41 meters deep, and underwater archaeologists have brought 30,000 objects from its depths. Today, it is a popular swimming hole. 21

acres around this well contained a double quadrangle of buildings, some with elaborate façade ornamentation and monolithic concrete construction. Pottery found here ranges from formative (200 B.C.) to the present day. The ruins here also include an old colonial church. There is a small museum where many of the artifacts are on display.

C2: In the opposite direction on highway 261 there are several excellent *Maya* sites. Just south of Muna you will find **Uxmal** and **Kabah**. However, you can turn east at Muna on highway 184 and go as far as Oxkutzcab. Here, a road south will take you past the Loltún cave and on to the ruins of **Labná**, **Xlapak** and **Sayil**. This road ends at highway 261 where you can turn north for the other two sites mentioned above before returning to Mérida. Obviously this "circle" route can be done the other way around if you wish. For descriptions of these sites, see Route 2-B.

C3: Southeast of Mérida lies the once-famous Maya city of **Mayapán**, now rather desolate. It is reached by the Tecoh-Telchaquillo road (Yuc 18). Follow Calle 67 to the divided highway which goes to the Outer Loop. Continue straight ahead. 22k/13m along the way, you will pass through **Acanceh**, with a small pyramid right on the main plaza.

The name in Maya means "the deer lament." These ruins were first studied by Edward Seler in 1905. Somewhat extensive excavations were carried out in 1941. This settlement probably existed from around 200 B.C. and lasted until the fifteenth century A.D. During the classic Maya period it was a great city, and was probably rebuilt during this time. The present pyramid, in poor condition, was the center of an acropolis. The original platform on which the pyramid stands was enlarged, and a second structure in palace form was built. It was covered with stucco and painted with scenes reminiscent of the art of **Teotihuacán**. Some remains of the stucco can still be seen on the side of the pyramid, which is now surrounded by a low wall with a wooden gate. The stairs and balustrades are in good condition and the four levels or tiers can easily be distinguished.

MAYAPÁN (Mah-yah-pahn': Daily, 8–5, Adm.) is about 40K/25M from Mérida.

Once one of the major *Maya* sites, Mayapán has been archaeologically neglected. E. M. Shook worked here from 1952–1955, and further work was done in 1962 by a group which included H. Pollock, R. Roys, T. Proskouriakoff and A. L. Smith. At its height Mayapán was a walled city containing 3,600 structures and more than 12,000 inhabitants. It was built in the Maya "renaissance" period and attempted to recapture some of the earlier Maya grandeur by using the corbelled vault, carved stucco, hieroglyphic writing, etc. The artisans were inferior, however, and even the pottery, mostly monochrome, is far less attractive, though it is technically superior. Most interesting are the large ceramic incense burners modeled as figures of the gods.

The Itzás settled in Mayapán in 987 A.D. and in the twelfth century formed a league with **Chichén-Itzá** and **Uxmal**. Around 1200 A.D. Mayapán under Nunac Ceel Canuch assumed the leadership of the league. Militarism arose, and eventually fighting broke out between the city-states. The Tutul-Xiu began a war against Mayapán and in 1441 the city was captured and partially destroyed. Today the visible remains are few. There is one temple pyramid in rather poor condition. A courtyard with columns is somewhat similar to the Temple of the Warriors at **Chichén-Itzá**, but on a much smaller scale. The structure near the entrance to the ruins has been called the Jaguar House, and one small round structure nearby, thought to be dedicated to Kukulkán, is a good example of the masonry of the period. It is hard to believe that at one time between eleven and twelve thousand people lived here. Most has been lost to the silence of the creeping vegetation.

Buses to Oxkutzcab pass by both these sites.

C4: East of Mérida lies the great center of **Chichén-Itzá**, a round trip of 240k/150m. There are departures daily at 8:45 from the ADO bus station on Calle 69 at 68, and hourly second class buses. By car you can also visit **Aké** and **Izamal**. For descriptions of these sites see Route 2-D.

In Mérida itself visit the fine Anthropological Museum on Paseo Montejo in the beautifully refurbished Palacio Montejo (Calle 56A near Calle 43 · Tue–Sun, 8–8; Adm).

2-D: MÉRIDA TO PUERTO JUÁREZ (322K/200M)

ADO buses leave hourly for Puerto Juárez and follow highway 180. For the motorist there is a somewhat more interesting route. Go east from Mérida on state highway 80 to Tixkokob (21k/13m). At the east end of town a road southeast leads to **Aké** (11k/7m). There is a large henniquen factory nearby. **Aké** can also be reached from highway 180 but the road is in poor condition.

This site was on the border between the old Maya states of Izamal and T'ho (Mérida today). It was a walled city and had a causeway to Izamal, 32k/20m away. The principle edifice here was called the Temple of the Warriors. There is a long platform with 36 columns 5.20 meters high, 1.30 thick in circular stone segments. In front is an immense stairway with steps 45 meters wide! Aké was a thriving city from 250 to 900 A.D.

Continue on 80 to Tekanto, turn south for 6k/4m to Citilcum and then east to **Izamal**. If you want to skip **Aké** Izamal can be reached by a road from Hoctun 48k/30m from Mérida on highway 180 (it is 24k/15m to the site), or Kantinul 16k/10m farther on (17k to Izamal).

This is the "place of the Itzás" and was flourishing between 850 and 1000 A.D. Nineteenth century explorers like J. L. Stephens (1843) and D. Charnay (1887) described this site. Sadly, most of the original grandeur is gone. I. Marquina worked here in 1951. According to *Maya* mythology, Votan sent his son Itzamná to civilize the region. When he died a temple was built over his grave and he was worshipped as Itzamatul, or "the spirit, the dew and the substance from heaven." He was also called Kabul or "celestial or creative hand." Red handprints became one of his symbols. Izamal itself became a large and important city and was still thriving when the Spaniards arrived. The main place was 200 by 300 meters, with a large pyramid structure on each side. When bishop Diego de Landa described the city, there were 11 or 12 stone pyramids with statues and palaces or temples on them. The remains of 5 of them can still be seen.

The base of the Kinich Kak Moo temple was the third largest ever built in Mesoamerica (195 by 173 meters, and 35 meters high) and the building had a number of colossal stucco heads on the substructure. The building was begun somewhere between 100 and 200 A.D. The Temple of Kabul had 20 stone steps more than 30 meters wide. The priest's house on another pyramid was replaced by the Franciscan convent. There are also the ruins of the great mausoleum which is said to contain the bones of Itzamná.

From Kantinul it is 60k/37.5m to **Chichén-Itzá** (daily, 8–5, Adm). An ADO bus leaves Mérida at 8:45 a.m. and there are second class buses hourly. Buses stop in Piste, one kilometer from the entrance. Buses from Cancún also stop here. You will need several hours to see all of the ruins. If possible, don't miss Chichén Viejo on the south side.

The name of this site means "at the mouth of the well of the Itzá." Dozens of archaeologists have visited and worked at this site. Sylvanus Morley spent 17 years here. The Carnegie Institute did notable work in 1924. The famous "cenote" or well was excavated by expert underwater archaeologists in 1960–61. Since dozens of descriptions and studies have been published, only some of the important historical and archaeological notes will be given here.

Around 400 A.D. farmers lived in this area near the wells. A tribe known as the Itzá settled in the area in 455 A.D. according to the

Popul Vuh. About a century and a half later, they abandoned the site (infertile land? unfriendly neighbors?) and moved to the coast, to the present city of Champotón. In 948 a move back to the site began, probably as part of the wave of *Toltec* peoples who migrated to the peninsula. By 987 the city was reestablished and the construction of many of the fine buildings now on the north side of the road took place. After the intra-Maya war from 1441–1461 (see **Mayapán**), the city was abandoned. Dates from some of the structures on the south side show that even when the Itzá were gone people lived in the area and Maya influence was felt there, as the architecture clearly shows. The archaeological zone is about three kilometers long and two wide. It was owned for a time by the American Consul, Edward Thompson, who brought up the first artifacts from the sacred well.

Some facts about the structures on the north side (the numbers in parentheses correspond to the accompanying map):

a) the Castle, or Pyramid of Kukulkán (2)—the original pyramid is underneath the present one which has nine tiers and is 24 meters high. The four stairways divide the sides into eighteen sections, for the eighteen months of the Maya calendar year. There are 90 steps on each side for a total of 360 days (the final five days belonged to no month). The serpents at the north stairway represent Kukulkán, the leader of the *Toltec* migration to the site, deified as Quetzalcoatl (the pyramid inside may be visited from 11 to 1 and from 4 to 5). At the time of the summer equinox the shadows of the steps form a snake whose stone head is at the bottom of the balustrade.

b) the Temple of the Warriors (3) is the last of three superimposed constructions and a replica of the temple at **Tula**. There are 60 columns in four rows, 2.60 meters high. The temple together with the courtyard of the 1,000 columns covers five acres. The longest side is 130 meters.

c) the market (5) covers 19.76 acres. The 25 columns are 4.75 meters high.

d) the sacred well (12) has yielded thousands of artifacts. Those given by Thompson to the Peabody Museum at Harvard University were returned to the Mexican government in 1959. The drop to the water's surface is 24 meters.

e) the tzompantli (8) with its face of sculptured skulls once had a wall standing on it which had the skulls of sacrificial victims on display in neat rows. The nearby platform was for sacrifices to the god of fire.

f) the ball court (11) sculptures depict scenes from the ball game, including the sacrifice of at least one of the losers. The rings are a little over a meter in diameter and six meters above the ground. On top of the north "tribune" is the Temple of the Bearded Man,

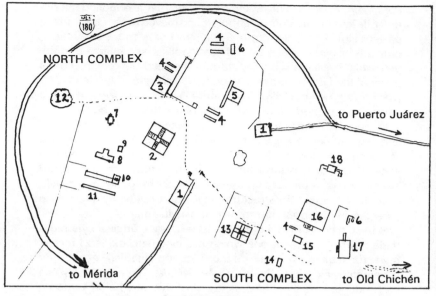

CHICHEN-ITZA

1. parking area
2. temple of Kukulkan or "castle"
3. temple of the warriors and court of 1,000 columns
4. ball courts
5. market
6. sweat houses
7. temple of Chac Mool
8. skull rack platform
9. platform of the eagles
10. temple of the tigers
11. great ball court
12. sacred sacrificial well
13. tomb of the high priest
14. house of the deer
15. colored (red) house
16. observatory (sometimes referred to as "caracol")
17. nuns' house or church
18. house of dark writing

another representation of Quetzalcoatl; the two columns are portrayals of rattlesnakes. The court is nearly 30 meters long—the largest one in Mesoamerica. The following structures are in the south group.

g) the Osarium (13) was a high priest's tomb; a pyramid was built over an underground cave which served as the burial chamber. E. Thompson removed the bones in 1896.

h) Chichan-Chob (15) means "colored house"; the lower tier is 20 × 17 × 5 meters.

i) the House of the Deer (14) was so called because there was a painting of one on a wall of an inner chamber.

k) the inner doorway of the Akab Tzib (Dark Writing—18) has red hands on the walls of the rooms on the west side, symbols of Itzamná.

l) the so-called Nuns' House (17—because its ten rooms reminded the Spaniards of a colonial convent) is covered with masks of the rain god. This is the old Maya Puuc style.

If you walk some distance south you will come to "Old Chichén" where you can see the remains of a phallic temple (dated 619 A.D.) and two other structures which show that the Maya from the south settled here. They later mixed with the Toltec-Itzá groups to form the so-called "second empire."

5k/3m east of Chichén-Itzá you will come to a dirt and gravel road (left) lined with whitewashed stones which takes you to the **Balankanché** (bah-lahn-kahn-chay') **Cave**, just a short distance away (daily 9–5, Adm. except Sun. Tours in groups only: in English at 11, 1 and 3).

The cave was discovered in 1959 by members of the National Institute of Anthropology and History. E. W. Andrews studied the site in 1961. This 800 meter cave was dedicated to the rain god and filled with ceremonial offerings. One chamber was filled with incense burners picturing Chac Mool or Tlaloc. Another had stone braziers and plates, grinding stones, pestles and other artifacts. In some places niches had been carved into the rock for statues, some of them a meter high. Dating has shown that some of these offerings were placed here around 870 A.D. This practice continued until at least the twelfth century. Near the cave entrance there is a small plaza with the remains of some stone structures.

Continuing east you will pass Nuevo X-Can. A paved road south goes to **Cobá** (52k/32m; see Route 2-E for a description). From here it is an easy drive to Puerto Juárez. If you are not going to follow Route 2-E, it is possible to take the ferry boat from here to both **Isla Mujeres** and **Cozumel**.

2-E: PUERTO JUÁREZ TO CHETUMAL (392K/245M)
Puerto Juárez is one of the departure points for two islands which are much better known as resorts than archaeological sites: **Isla Mujeres** and **Cozumel**. Both, however, have vestiges of *Maya* remains. From the port a "people ferry" leaves 9 times a day for the forty minutes ride to **Isla Mujeres** (ees'lah moo-hay'-res). There is a car ferry from Punta Sam every two hours from 7 a.m. to 10 p.m.

The island was named by the Spanish explorer Hernández de Córdoba who landed there in 1517 and found a quantity of feminine figurines. These were votive offerings, probably for fertility, at the shrine of Ixchel. This is on the southern tip of the island, 500 meters from the ruins of what is thought to have been a Maya observatory. Much of these structures was destroyed by a hurricane in 1988. There are several mounds on the island.

It wasn't until 1975 that the last incomplete stretches of highway 307 were finished, opening up to tourists the whole beautiful world of the Caribbean coast of the Yucatán peninsula. There are dozens of archaeological sites in this area, and as the tourist trade increases, more of them will be made accessible to the traveler. Some, formerly reached only by light aircraft, are now right on the highway, or a short distance from it.

Cancún, only two miles south of Puerto Juárez, has become a major beach resort, with an international airport. Buses leave Mexico City 7 times a day for Cancún from the east terminal. There are two parts to Cancún. One is a long spit of land which forms a beautiful lagoon between itself and the mainland in a "7" shape. At the bend of the peninsula is Cancún's Convention Center where the Anthropology Museum is located. It was badly damaged by the hurricane in 1988 and is temporarily closed, but should be open again some time in 1992. The "peninsula" is now a line of hotels along Kukulkán Boulevard. As you drive this road, at k12, on the lagoon side opposite the Sheraton Hotel, there is a site known as **Yamil Lu'um**, found by Stephens in his 1840's explorations. There are two small structures (temples?) with traces of Maya paintings. At k16.5 the still untouched ruins of San Miguelito can be found, and 1/2k farther on, a road (r) leads to the **Ruinas del Rey** (daily, 8–5, Adm).

This center had a plaza with structures on three sides and included a pyramid with a temple on top. Another temple had two corridors and wall paintings. The platforms lining this one-street town have columns which sustained the roofs of the buildings on them. This was a port of commercial control and was active between 1300 and 1400 A.D.

In Cancún itself, there are agencies which organize daytrips to **Tulum** and **Cobá** to the south, and west to **Chichén-Itzá**. Viajes Bojórquez (12 Alcatraces St.; tel. 7-11-56) is one of the best. In the hotel zone, try VISA Tours at Plaza Quetzal (3-18-00). Buses ADC and ADO leave 4 to 6 times a day for Chetumal, stopping at **Tulum**. "Transportes de Oriente" also covers portions of this route. Puerto Juárez is only 15 minutes away by bus for trips to **Isla Mujeres** and **Cozumel**. Take the Ruta 8 bus going north on Avenida Tulum.

36k/23m farther south on highway 307 is Puerto Morelos, a departure point for **Cozumel** island, especially if you plan to take your car. Four days a week you have to be ready to leave by 6 a.m.! (10 on Thurs and

Sat; no trip Sun). The boat trip from Playa del Carmen 32k/20m farther on is much shorter. In addition to the regular ferry boat (5 times a day) there is a hydrofoil service. Cozumel also has an international airport. Like Cancún it has long been a favorite vacation and tourist resort, a radical change from its Pre-Columbian purpose.

Cozumel (ko-soo-mell') is a corruption of cutzamil, or "land of swallows." This island, 19k/12m from the mainland, is 45k/28m long and 15k/9.5m wide at the widest point. This was one of the first sites visited by the Spaniards in 1518 and 1519. It was a center of pilgrimage during the classic *Maya* period (to the temple of Ixchel, the moon goddess), and an important trade port, especially during the Mayapán period. During 1972 an archaeological project by J. and P. Sabloff, W. Rathje, D. Friedl and J. Connor identified 33 sites on the island, most of them at the northern end, near Aguada Grande. Walls have been found which may indicate a division of land and property ownership. Remains of the Maya observatory at the southern end of the island include an arch and columns with capitals. A little over half way across the south road a dirt road (left, going east) leads to El Cedral. The Ixchel temple, at the center of the island in the San Gervasio group (daily, 8–5, Adm) is fairly easy to reach. 14k/9m along the highway across the island an unpaved road (1) goes to the site. You can rent a bike in San Miguel, and it is possible to hire a taxi and make a circuit of the island which includes several sites.

Between Playa del Carmen and the town of Akumal there are several sites on the sea side of the highway, but presently only one is accessible: Xcaret (shkah'-ret) about 4k/2.5m south. A road (left) at a restaurant on the highway leads 1k to the site entrance. The ruins are a short walk toward the sea.

This little-known *Maya* site was investigated by E. W. Andrews in 1955–56, and by W. T. Sanders in 1960. It is a walled town of the late period, and was on the pilgrimage route from the interior of Yucatán to the sacred island of Cozumel. Remains include those of a small pyramid with a doorway on top; a small vaulted shrine, and a two-room building with a round doorway. Many buildings of this port city lie hidden in the surrounding jungle.

At Puerto Aventuras (26k/16m from Xcaret) there is a very unusual museum (daily, 8–5, Adm). Its showcases are filled with objects which have been found by underwater archaeology along the coast, at Cozumel, and even at Chichén-Itzá and Chinkultic. These used to be at Xel-Ha—24k/15m farther south—now famous as a scuba diving center. The ruins of Xel-Ha are just a bit south of the diving center. A road (right) from the highway takes you to them. The visible structures (lots of hidden ones under the surrounding vegetation) include the Temple of the Jaguar, the Temple of the Birds (faint traces of the original art are still visible) and what may have been a market area. Continuing south on 307 about 5 minutes from Xel-Ha watch for a crude wooden sign on the left side of the road. It indicates the site of **Tancah** (tahn-kah') and is spelled backwards! This is another as yet untouched site.

Tancah is one of several *Maya* coastal sites occupied from around 300 A.D. until the arrival of the Spaniards. The construction activity took place mainly between 300 and 500 A.D. The site was described by S. Lothrop in 1924, I. Marquina in 1951 and W. T. Sanders in 1960. The center was surrounded by hamlets and clusters of houses, and itself was a ceremonial site. There remains a pyramid, with structures, and some columns. It had some excellent murals of the gods of corn and rain, discovered by Dr. A. Miller, but these were later looted.

From here it is a short run to **Tulum**, a unique site in many ways. You can reach Tulum directly from Mexico City on ADO buses which leave 4 times a day from the east terminal, and there are buses several times a day from Cancún's second class bus station.

Tulum (too-loom': 8–5, Adm. except Sun) means "wall" or "fortification." Originally it was probably Zama, or "dawn" and became known as "the city of dawn." Jerónimo Aguilar and Gonzalo Guerrero, two sixteenth-century Spanish adventurers, were kept as slaves here. Juan José Gálvez discovered the site in colonial times, and J. L. Stephens came upon it in 1848. Because of the caste wars during the nineteenth century, no archaeological work was done. S. Morley worked here four times between 1913 and 1922, and the Carnegie Institute had archaeologists here from 1916–1922. Miguel Angel Fernández has been investigating the site since 1938. Later investigators were I. Marquina (1951) and W. T. Sanders (1960).

The center was built between 564 and 593 A.D. and was a planned city containing fifty structures. Later it was completely closed in on three sides by walls covering 800 meters, which were 3 × 3 to 5 meters thick and high. The east has the Caribbean sea, 12 meters below the cliffs on which the site stands. The main area within this enclosure was 400 × 170 meters and contained some sixty structures. They are different from most other *Maya* types. There are no "pyramids" as such; temples are on platforms. The so-called "castle" was constructed in three stages. It was first a building of two rooms, then a two-room structure was built on top of this and decorated with niches and stucco figures. Two small temples flanked the stairway. The temple of the frescoes occupied the center of the ceremonial

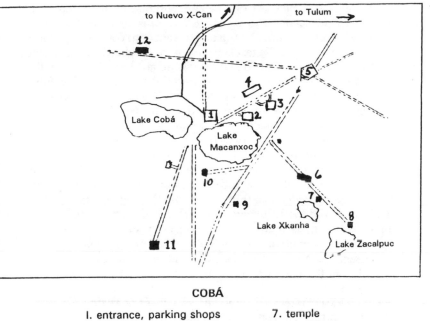

to Nuevo X-Can
to Tulum

Lake Cobá
Lake Macanxoc
Lake Xkanha
Lake Zacalpuc

COBÁ

1. entrance, parking shops	7. temple
2. Cobá group	8. Zacakal
3. Las Pinturas group	9. Lab Mul
4. ball court	10. Uitzil Mul
5. Nohuch Mul	11. Kitamná
6. Maxcanoc	12. Chacne

sacbes (Mayan roads)

group. There are murals in the subterranean rooms. The large stucco masks at the corners are representations of Itzmaná (see **Izamal**). This was built around 1263 A.D. The mural remains in the temple of the descending sun seem to be related to *Mixtec* art. Other structures include a funeral platform, a large palace, and a few other temples. In classic and post-classic times, Tulum was the major port of trade for most of the Maya centers on the Yucatán peninsula.

1½m south of here a road right leads (42k/26m) to **Cobá** (ko-bah'). For a long time accessible only by air, muleback and a very bad road, this striking Maya center has become a major tourist attraction (8–5, Adm). There were 78,000 visitors here in 1990. Buses from Tulum pass here twice a day on their way to Valladolid (and vice-versa). A taxi from Tulum is about $15.00 round trip with 2 hours for visiting. Organized tours leave from Cancún (and even Mérida). Check with Intermar Caribe at Ceriza and Bonampak streets.

The original name was Cobá-Kinchil, and may mean "screeching grouse." This classic *Maya* center (623 A.D.) is set amid five small lakes, and had more than 40 causeways (sacbeoh) connecting it with outlying centers. The longest is 96k/60m to **Yaxuná**. The city developed during the early period and is related artistically to the southern Maya cities. It became a commercial center for jade from Guatemala, among other things. Eventually, the city and surrounding area covered 80 square kilometers and had 50,000 inhabitants. 6,500 structures have been identified, 4,000 in the city itself.

The first report of this site was from T. Maler in 1891. The Carnegie Institute worked here from 1926 to 1930, and J. E. Thompson reported on the site in 1932. From 1972 to 1975 excavations were supervised by E. Valencia and the area was surveyed and mapped.

It has been divided into three areas: the Cobá group, the Nohoch Mul group and the Chucmuc Mul group. The Cobá group, to the right just past the entrance, has temples, platforms, rooms with patios and a pyramid (called "iglesia") 24 meters high of nine tiers, in the Petén, Guatemala art style. The Nohoch Mul group, straight ahead from the entrance and left at a fork, has two of the major structures: a pyramid 42 meters high with a central stairway 11 meters wide (120 steps), divided into seven sections with a temple at the top, and the remains of a platform 120 × 124 meters and 30 meters high, with evidences of houses on it. The ball court was an impressive one. The third group (also called Las Pinturas) is to the right of the fork in the path. Its main attraction is a pyramid with painted lintels. Throughout the ruins 32 stelae have been found, one of them with 313 hieroglyphs on it. Dates on these vary from 610 to 684 A.D. One of the most intriguing finds was a huge roller for surface leveling, weighing 5 tons.

Back on highway 307, the road turns toward an immense swamp area. Amazingly enough, traces of at least seventeen sites have been found in this region. An enormous area has been set aside as a Biosphere Reserve, called Sian Ka'an. Within it, two sites about 28k/17m from Tulum, **Muyil** and **Chunyaxché** are fairly close to the highway. They probably formed part of a larger complex. The sites are not yet easily accessible, but the adventuresome should find them interesting.

Chunyaxché (choon-yash-chay') was explored by Michel Peissel in the 1960's. Situated on an inland lagoon, this city may date back to the early part of the first century A.D. and have been one of the most important in the area. 108 buildings have been identified, including several palaces. The main pyramid is larger than that of **Tulum**. Some are structures along a road (sacbe) which joined this center with **Muyil** (moo-yeel') which may have served as a commercial center and port. Explored in 1926 by H. Spinden and G. Mason, it is still virtually untouched. Tulane University has worked here in recent years with the state branch of the National Institute of Anthropology and History under archaeologist Elía del Carmen. Twelve temples and ceremonial buildings have been identified, all from late classic *Maya* civilization.

The only city of any size along this highway is Felipe Carrillo Puerto. From here, highway 184 cuts diagonally across the peninsula 232k/145m and joins highway 261 and Route 2-B 62k/40m south of Mérida. Continuing south on 307, about 38k/24m from Chetumal you will come to Lake Bacalar—a vast expanse of celestial blue that is breathtaking. On this lake shore is the little town of Bacalar, where a fort built in 1733 now houses a little museum (9–5) with a number of archaeological pieces, the only collection of this kind in the whole region. There are hourly buses from Chetumal.

2-F: CHETUMAL TO ESCÁRCEGA (273K/170M)

The dense forests of the southern part of the Yucatán peninsula hide the remains of dozens of former *Maya* centers. Four are easily accessible from the highway. Many of the others can be visited by jeep, on horseback, or on foot, but a guide is indispensable. The Mexican Tourist Office in Chetumal can help you make arrangements, or suggest agencies which will do so.

52k/32m west of Chetumal on highway 186 you will come to a hardpacked, white gravel road to the left. This will take you 12k/7.5m to the impressive pyramid of **Kohunlich** (ko-hoon-leech').

There are remains of some fifty structures in this "place of the fruitful date trees." The most important one is the pyramid which is unique for the huge stucco masks which decorate the three-tiered façade, on either side of the central stairway. They were very similar to the ones described by Landa and drawn by Catherwood at **Izamal**. Work has been done at this late pre-classic site (dating from 300 B.C.) by V. Segovia, and the ball court, the stelae building and part of the irrigation system are now visible.

Some 48k/30m farther west on 186 you will come to the village of **Xpujil** (shpoo-heel'). ADO buses from Mexico City's east terminal stop here 3 times a day. The ruins are visible from the highway, to the right.

This site was reported by K. Ruppert and J. H. Denison in 1943, by I. Marquina in 1951, and by A.M. Tozzer in 1957. It existed from 400 to 900 A.D., although monochrome pottery of the Chicanel style found here indicates a much earlier settlement. What the visitor sees today are the remains of a building in the Río Bec style, the two false towers with part of their crests. The 12 sections each contain a room; the façade of the center structure has a niche with serpent heads around it. Archaeology has hardly scratched the surface at this *Maya* center.

Only 12k/7.5m farther on, a dirt road to the right takes you to the ruins of **Becán**, about 200 meters from the highway and surrounded by massive trees. Sometimes there are children around who will guide you through the unbelievable maze of underground rooms for a few pesos (8–5, Adm)

Becán (bay-kahn') was discovered by K. Ruppert of the Carnegie Institute in 1934, and subsequently studied by E. W. Andrews in 1943, A. Ruz in 1945, and most recently by Richard Adams in 1970 and 1973 under the auspices of the National Geographic Society. This *Maya* city existed from early classic times and was attacked around 450 A.D. For protection, the inhabitants dug a trench around the city varying in width from three to twenty-four meters, and in depth from two to four meters. It was 1.2 miles in circumference and had seven bridges across it. Some historians consider this one of the earliest fortified sites in Middle America, and perhaps a sign of institutionalized militarism. The site is composed of structures (temples, palaces) grouped around plazas. There are remains of a ball court, and at least four stelae have been found. One interesting feature is the variation in the sizes of rooms, indicating class distinctions. The distinctive feature is the style of architecture known as **Río Bec** with the tall, false corner towers, ornamented with small temples on top of them. Dense vegetation covers much of this site, but some of the monumental staircases can be seen, and also some of the fine stonework on the façades of the buildings. The largest mound is honeycombed with a labyrinth of rooms on various levels.

3.2k/2m west of **Becán** on the left side of the highway there is a road which leads to the ruins of **Chicanná** (chee-kah-nah').

These ruins were discovered (1966), named and partially excavated during three seasons beginning in 1974 by Jack Eaton, and by A. Peña in 1979. The most imposing feature of the site is a one-story eight room "palace" (known as Structure II) with an enormous and elaborate monster mask façade, a symbol of Itzamná (see **Izamal**). The building, a mixture of **Río Bec** and Chenes styles, is covered with stone and stucco sculpture. Each of the eight rooms has a raised bench of stone, and the five outside rooms have cord holders on either side of the doorway to hang a cloth for privacy. G. F. Andrews calls this an "elite residence," and it was at its height between 660 and 680 A.D. The south face of Structure XX underwent restoration in 1984, and two other structures have been rebuilt.

From this area (the crossroads at Xpujil) there is a jeep road through the forest to the ruins of **Río Bec**, the center which gave its name to the architectural style that predominates throughout the lower *Maya* regions. The road of some 40k/25m is difficult and should not be attempted without a guide.

Río Bec comprises ten groups of buildings scattered over an area of some fifty square kilometers. It was visited and studied by K. Ruppert and J. H. Denison in 1943, and many explorations have taken place since. The particular kind of architecture in the region has given its name to a style which has been found elsewhere in the *Maya* world. It is characterized by a) long, low structures giving the impression of being divided into three buildings, each with a serpent-mouth door, and a façade decorated with columns, geometric designs in stonework and masks; b) tall corner towers ornamented with small steep steps and miniature temples on top; c) single wall roof combs, usually perforated; d) complex moldings. The temple pyramid is rare in this area.

From the road to **Chicanná** it is 150k/94m drive to Francisco Escárcega where you join Route 2-B. But—**warning!**—over the years this highway has become badly damaged and neglected. It is now in very bad shape and even at 30 mph is rough and difficult. It would almost be better to make the above-mentioned sites a daytrip from Chetumal and return to western Yucatán via highway 184, 39k/24m north of Chetumal, to Muna and the towns mentioned in Route 2-B, giving you the opportunity to visit the archaeological sites in that area, especially if you arrived in Mérida or Cancún via Route 2-A/D or directly by air.

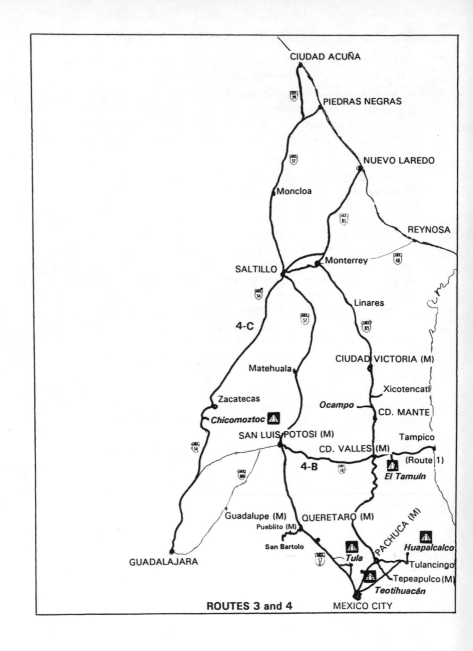

ROUTES 3 and 4

Route 3: The Pan-American Highway to Mexico City (1219k/757m)

The Pan-American highway (85) is one of the oldest travel routes, but it gets far less use than it did in the past, at least from Monterrey on because the central highway is much easier driving. The highway as far as Ciudad Valles is relatively easy, though parts of it are also somewhat mountainous. Between Ciudad Valles and Actopan the road resembles the tortuous twists of an oversized snake. While the highway has sections of scenery which are absolutely awesome in their splendor, these same portions of the road are filled with hairpin turns, sharp curves, countless blind spots and, at certain times of the day, a veil of fog. There are many places along the endlessly winding road where the dropoff is several hundred feet. Occasional crosses along the side of the road are reminders that someone wasn't driving carefully. If you are willing to drive leisurely (35 to 40 mph) this route has much of real beauty in it.

For bus travelers, the bus station in Nuevo Laredo is at the western edge of town and can be reached by a city bus or taxi (ask for "la camionera central"—la kah-mee-yone air' ah sen trahl'). Many bus lines go to Monterrey, but most of the long-distance buses use the central highway (Route 4), so to get past Monterrey you will have to look for a bus line which goes to Ciudad Victoria, Ciudad Mante or Ciudad Valles. From these places buses to Mexico City follow the Pan-American route.

Monterrey is the first large city on this route. Once a pleasant, modern city with lingering colonial charm, Monterrey has been socked in by the pollution of the enormous industrial complexes which have grown up in and around it. The famous saddle mountain, once a landmark, can barely be seen through the heavy smog. There is a museum which can be found in the old bishop's palace on a hill at the west side of the town (Calle Obispo Vergel) but it is dedicated mainly to artifacts and events of colonial and independent Mexico.

The drive from here to Linares and Ciudad Victoria is fairly pleasant though it has little to offer archaeologically. Ciudad Victoria (which can be bypassed by taking the road to the left at the edge of town) has a museum which is located on Hnos. Vásquez between Matamoros and

71

Morelos, in one of the State University buildings (Mon-Fri, 9–1, 2–7; Sat, Sun 9–1). There are some very good *Huastec* pieces.

40k/25m south of this city you will cross the Tropic of Cancer. There is a monument on the left side of the road (an orange-colored concrete ball). 12k/7m farther on the road (left) to Ignacio Zaragoza is a good shortcut to Tampico and Route 1.

Archaeological maps indicate two sites between Ciudad Victoria and Ciudad Mante. One is Xicontencatl. Artifacts have been found here, but there are no visible ruins in or near the village. A few miles farther on, a road to the right (42k/26m) goes to **Ocampo** (oh-kahm'-po).

This is basically a cave site which was explored and excavated in 1958 by R. MacNeish. Incipient stem dart points, flakes and scrapers show that the cave was inhabited between 5000 and 3000 B.C. Checker-woven and twilled mats and baskets date from 3604 and 3244 B.C. Seventy to eighty per cent of the food was based on the simple collection of plants. The site is important as an excellent example of a Mexican counterpart to the European mesolithic period. 4k east of the city in Parque de la Alberca there is a small pyramid and other remains of an early culture. There is a museum in town with *Huastec* artifacts.

When you reach Ciudad Valles, continue through town on 85. Just before you reach the monument of jetting fountains, watch for José Peñalosa street (right). Three blocks down this street you will come to a red brick building at the corner of Rotaros. Turn right, and you are at the entrance of the Joaquín Meade Regional Museum (Mon–Fri, 9–1, 3–6). Señora Oralia Gutiérrez de Sánchez spent 45 years bringing together this fascinating collection. The animal and human clay figurines are especially noteworthy. Well worth the detour. Back on highway 85, a short distance farther south you will come to highway 70 where you can join Route 4-B and visit the *Huastec-Totonac* center of **Tamuín.**

Continuing south from Ciudad Valles the next portion of the drive toward Mexico City is what is described in the first paragraph of this Route. Eventually you will come to Pachuca. At Arista and Hidalgo streets you will find the old Franciscan convent now the Regional Museum of Hidalgo (Tue–Sat, 10–2, 5–7; Sun 10–2). It is a surprisingly good museum with information and artifacts covering much of the area's Pre-Columbian history and compensates for the lack of sites to visit. Pachuca can be reached on Autobuses Unidos from Mexico City's east terminal, or ADO which leaves every 15 minutes from the north terminal.

If you do not go into town but take the "loop" around it, there are three possible exits. The first takes you back to highway 85 south to Mexico City. Watch for signs indicating where you can double back toward **Teotihuacán** (see Route 5-Ca for details) if you wish to. The second is a road to Ciudad Sahagún. On this road, not far from Zempoala (there is a fascinating colonial aqueduct visible from the road) you will come to a crossroad. Turn right to go to **Teotihuacán** and Mexico City. If you continue straight on toward Ciudad Sahagún, at its outskirts a road left goes to Tepeapulco. On Av. Hidalgo, on top of what was a temple to the god Huitzilopoztli, the Franciscans built a convent. Today it houses a three-room museum of artifacts from around the pyramid of nearby Jiquingo and the archaeological zone of El Tecolote (Wed-Sun, 10–2, 4–6; Adm). The third exit is to highway 136 east. 46k/29m farther on is the town of Tulancingo. At the east end of town on a road north (left) 3k/1.5m away are the ruins of **Huapalcalco**. The site is visible some 150 meters up from the road. César Lizardi worked here in 1959. There is one small restored pyramid and some vestiges of a tomb and other structures. This was one of the early *Toltec* sites.

Returning west through Tulancingo, about 9k/5m from town a road south (left) goes directly to **Teotihuacán** and Mexico City.

Route 5 covers all of the archaeological sites in and around Mexico City.

Route 4: The Central Highways

The central highways of Mexico are major travel routes to both Mexico City and Guadalajara. The highway to Mexico City (85, 40, 57) is not much shorter than the Pan American highway (Route 3), but it is much easier driving and, though far less scenic, offers the archaeological site of **Tula** and the museums in San Luis Potosí and Querétaro, with some interesting possible side trips.

The northern part of this route lies in the state of Coahuila (ko-ah-wee'-lah). This is Mexico's third largest state. It has vast tracts without rivers or water, and in general is thinly populated. Secondary mountain ranges run through the state, and many caves have been found in them, several with traces of occupation: Ramírez Cave, Peñón Angosto Cave, and especially Frightful Cave. This region was the home of nomadic tribes generally known as Coahuiltecans. They ranged all across the north and into present-day United States, particularly Texas. They developed what has been called a "Desert Culture," which existed as early as 7500 B.C. No large, major cultural complex has been found, but some inhabited sites have been identified: Nadadores, Sacramento, Paila and the previously mentioned caves, to name a few. W. W. Taylor who has studied this region uses the term "tethered nomadism," meaning that the people were nomads, but were also "tied to" their caves, so that they did not roam for great distances once they had found a "home." The artifacts which have been found have all been of basic raw materials: stone, wood, bone, shell and plant fibers. Quite a few cave drawings have been discovered, but it is difficult to identify them chronologically, because the Indian groups in Texas also roamed into Mexico as late as 1850.

Among the groups which seem to have originated in this general region are the *Otomí* tribes. The name of this group means "bird arrows" and it describes, in a way, the life-style of this nomadic tribe that inhabited the north central highlands of Mexico, on the fringes of Mesoamerica. They followed a simple hunting and gathering way of life, and even as late as 900 A.D. some of them were still living in caves. Others eventually settled down to an agricultural life and developed a simple ceramic tradition. Basically a warlike group, they moved southward between 100 and 500 A.D. perhaps eventually mingling with the *Chichimecs* and taking part in the attacking and burning of **Teotihuacán** around 650 A.D. Tradition says that an Otomí leader married a Chichimec princess and settled in Xaltocan, but this little kingdom fell to the Tepanecs of Azcapotzalco. Others settled in Cuauhtitlán and extended their dominion around 800 A.D. to the Toluca, Mezquital and central Anáhuac valleys. Later on, one branch of the Otomí tribe joined the *Toltecs* and became part of the empire that ruled from **Tula**.

The cultural traits of the Otomí included tatooing, tooth blackening, worship of the fire god and the moon, and the use of hallucinogenic mushrooms for divination. With the rise of the powerful states around Lake Texcoco, Otomí unity dissolved and they were incorporated into other groups. Small, isolated pockets of their descendents live in the mountain regions of San Luis Potosí and Querétaro.

4-A: LAREDO/NUEVO LAREDO TO MEXICO CITY (1177K/734M)

Highway 85 is part of the original Pan American highway. For this route it is taken as far as Monterrey. There are numerous bus lines from Nuevo Laredo to Mexico City or any of the major cities along the route. (Check the beginning of Route 3 for details). If you don't want to stop in Monterrey look for "directo" posted on the bus schedules. They bypass the town. You can bypass the city also 16k/10m north of it; the sign reads "Saltillo."

In Monterrey there is a museum in the old bishop's palace on a hill at the west end of town on Calle Obispo Vergel, but it has little of Pre-Columbian interest (Tue-Fri, 9:30-5; Sat, Sun 10:30-6). Not far from there the central highway turns west and becomes highway 40 which will take you to Saltillo which you can also bypass by looking for the indications of highway 57 which comes from the border towns of Del Rio/Ciudad Acuña and Eagle Pass/Piedras Negras from which you can also take Route 4. There are buses from these cities also to Saltillo (or Monterrey) where you can change to a bus for Mexico City. "Anahuac" has service from both border cities to Mexico City.

It is a long drive (about 5 hours) to the first major city which is San Luis Potosí. After you pass Matehuala, and just before you get to San Gabriel, you will cross the Tropic of Cancer. Nothing around you looks "tropical" unless you are thinking of some desert areas of Africa. The greenery of San Luis Potosí is a welcome sight. To get to the museum in this city, go one block west past the main plaza to Aldama street, turn left and go three blocks to Galeana. Turn right, and the museum is toward the end of the block in the old Franciscan convent (now painted an ugly orange-red. Tue-Sat, 10-2, 4-6; Sun 10-2:30; Adm). There are two good archaeological maps of the state (of San Luis Potosí) and several halls of fine exhibits. The museum features especially the *Huastecs* who inhabited the eastern part of the state, the *Otomí* and other central Mexican groups along with the Rioverde cultures.

From here it is 204k/127m to Querétaro. Highway 57 enters the city at the west end. Signs indicate the way to the center of town and the main plaza. The bus station is on Zaragoza street, about five blocks south of this plaza. If you go north on Corregidora street, next to the church on the corner of the plaza is the regional museum. Much of it is devoted to nineteenth century history (independence and Maximilian), but there are some Pre-Hispanic artifacts, particularly of the *Tarascan* culture. Many of the archaeological finds from nearby Pueblito are housed here (Tue–Sun, 10–4:30; Adm). For a side trip to Pueblito's museum and archaeological site see Route 8-A.

Highway 57D to Mexico City is an excellent toll road, but before you get to the first toll gates, at 52k/35m from Querétaro there is an exit to San Juan del Río. Behind the church of El Panteón de la Santa Veracruz you will find a small museum featuring the local Pre-Columbian cultures, like the ceramics from El Rosario and La Cruz. But stop only if you have some extra time. However, if you are a real archaeology buff, there is a truly wonderful site way off the regular routes, but with paved road all the way. The total distance is 111k/70m. If you feel enticed, then from San Juan del Río take highway 120 north to Tequisquiapan; continue on to Ezequiel Montes, east to Cadereyta and north again to La Culata. Here a road east will take you to San Joaquín. The ruins of **Ranas y Toluquilla** are 3k away. They are very similar to **El Tajín** and **Xochicalco**. There are 53 buildings, some pyramids and a unique ball court.

Back on highway 57, at kilometer 83.5 a sign indicates the road to Jilotepic and **Tula**. There is another indication at kilometer 69, at the turnoff to the town of Tepeji. Either way will take you to the *Toltec* capital of **Tula**. Since it is only 69k/43m from Mexico City, you may want to come back here another day if you do not have time to stop at the moment. If you do, the Tepeji road is shorter. Go to the first intersection and turn left toward Tula. It is 24k/15m to the ruins on a hill just outside of the town, and there is a paved road to the entrance of the archaeological zone. (Tue–Sun, 10–6; Adm. except Sun.).

The original name, Tollán (toe-yahn') means "metropolis" in *Otomí* language and "gifted artisans" if it is a *Toltec-Chichimec* word. Fragments of some of the famous sculptured stone statues were found in 1873, and D. Charnay identified houses in 1880. In 1938 W. Jiménez Moreno correctly indicated the site as the center of the *Toltec* civilization and J. Acosta excavated here over a period of 20 years.

The history of the *Toltecs* that has come down to us is perhaps a little too "neat" and exact to be taken literally, since it speaks of ten kings from 856 to 1168, which happens to be 312 years, or six cycles of 52 years. The Toltec civilization was certainly at its peak during those years, but it started much earlier, and probably did not fall into a series of equal divisions. These are interesting, however, because they show that this group held the belief that the sun was reborn every 52 years, and life started over again. This included the rebuilding of pyramids.

Between 300 and 600 A.D. Nahua speaking groups left **Teotihuacán** and moved to the gulf coast, the Pacific coast and to the south. Between 600 and 900 these dispersed groups began uniting. Some of them had experienced the influence of **El Tajín** and the *Maya* cultures. They had also become warlike. Those that had settled in **Xochicalco** moved into the central Anáhuac valley and made their capital at the Cerro de la Estrella just outside of present-day Mexico City. From here they moved northeast to Tulancingo, and then west to Tollán, or present day **Tula**. The legendary leader of this migration was Mixcohautl-Mazatzin. Around 900 they were joined by a group of Pipiles or Nonoalcas who had migrated from Central America to the gulf coast of Mexico and then to the central highland valley. They brought with them the knowledge of metallurgy.

Toltec civilization began to rise under Ce-Acatl-Topiltzin who was the ninth king of Tollán in 960. Tula became "the Athens of Anáhuac". The sloping sides of the ball court were changed to high walls with stone rings. Columns were used as a means of creating a large inner space. Monumental sculpture was made, particularly the huge statues of the spear throwers. This king, who advanced the arts and sciences, became identified with the god Quetzalcoatl who had first brought this knowledge to humans. Legend says that he fell into sexual misconduct and was either banished from or voluntarily left Tula in 987 and became the leader of a group of Toltecs who migrated to the Yucatán peninsula and mixed with groups there to bring about the *Maya* renaissance. In this role he was known as Kukulkán, and the main pyramid at **Chichén-Itzá** is dedicated to him. The architecture there is also striking similar to that of Tula, a proof of Toltec influence. In any case, even though Ce-Acatl had left Tula, he was still remembered as the Morning Star, and a temple was built to him under that title. Some historians say that he was the seventh of eight kings to be identified with the god Quetzalcoatl, and that the first of the line was considered a reincarnation of the god himself. This would indicate that the cult to Quetzalcoatl had a fairly long tradition among the Toltecs and give some weight to a *Huastec* origin of the cult. The five-tiered temple in the north group of buildings was dedicated to him. The original structure was completely covered with sculptured panels of jaguars and eagles. Some of these are still in place. Sculptured warriors, 4.60 meters tall and made in four sections, supported the roof of the temple. They have stylized butterflies as breastplates, and feathered serpents on their sandals. All of these things later became symbols of Quetzalcoatl. Adjoining the temple pyramid is a palace and a hall of columns in three rows with 42 in each row, measuring 54 meters. The north group of ruins also has some sunken patios with decorated rooms and a statue of Chac Mool (the rain god) as a reclining figure, head turned to one side. The temple pyramid of the sun, on the east side of the plaza, was destroyed in 1168. The south group of ruins includes a plaza, the base of the temple pyramid, two palaces and Mound "C". There are ball courts in both groups, in the "I" form. Another group known as "El Corral" has one structure of combined rectangular and semicircular base, which had a temple to the wind god. It also had an altar with skulls and crossbones. This object, and representations of Izapapalotl or "Obsidian Butterfly," the god of sacrifice and death, indicate that many of the religious practices associated with the Aztecs actually began with or were refined by the Toltecs.

Between 1098 and 1156 king Huémoc extended the Toltec empire and influence to the east to such centers as **Teotihuacán**, Tulancingo and **Castillo del Teayo**, and to the south Cuernavaca and **Cholula**. In 1156 bands of raiding *Chichimecs* attacked Tula and the people began to emigrate. Some went to Cholula and served under the historic Olemcs until they were strong enough to overthrow their masters and take the city, around 1170. Others went to the Yucatán peninsula to join the Itzá. Still others settled in the Lake Texcoco region, founding Colhuacán, Tepanec and Azcapotzalco.

Continuous raids by the *Chichimecs* finally brought the Toltec empire to an end with the destruction of Tula in 1168. When the Toltecs dispersed they took many of their customs with them and these became diffused throughout Mexico. Of importance was the worship of various gods, especially Chac Mool or Tlaloc (rain) and the gods of war and the sky. The Quetzalcoatl cult, of course, remained strong. Along with this worship went the bloody act of human sacrifice and the skull racks. The military trappings—clubs inset with obsidian blades and quilted "armor"—were also adopted by other groups. The presence of the skull rack near the second ball court is evidence that the *Aztecs* reinhabited the area for a time. On an entirely different note, the Toltecs have been credited with popularizing pulque, the strong alcoholic drink made from the maguey plant, since, according to legend, it was the Toltec princess Xochitl who revealed the secret of making it.

There is a museum at the entrance to the ruins with good Toltec sculptures.

Leaving the site, continue straight ahead on the paved road. This is a short-cut to highway 57D. It is about an hour's drive to Mexico City. At kilometers 22 (actually on Avenida Toluca in Tlalnepantla) there is a turn-off to **Tenayuca** and Jardines de **Santa Cecilia** (see Route 5-B3, a, b). For the archaeological sites in and around Mexico City see Route 5.

4-B: SAN LUIS POTOSÍ TO TAMPICO (400K/249M)

From San Luis Potosí on the central highway 57 it is possible to join either Route 3 at Ciudad Valles, or Route 1 at Tampico by taking highway 70 east. This whole region is rich in archaeological sites, but few of them are near the regular highway route. Rioverde (131k/81m) for instance was an old *Otomí* site, and pottery and artifacts have been found in the vicinity. There are two or three sites near Santa Catarina, also, for those who might want to do some inquiring and exploring, and quite far off the route there is the extraordinary site of **Ranas y Toluquilla.** You must go south from Río Verde to Jalpan and west on highway 120 to the San Joaquín turnoff. This involves driving some of the world's curviest roads. (See Route 4-A for some details).

In Ciudad Valles the Joaquín Meade Regional Museum on 623 Rotaros has artifacts from four cultures in the Huasteca region and is well worth a visit (see Route 3 for details). 14k/9m east of Ciudad Valles you come to a sign indicating the resort hotel of Taninul. 2k down this road there is a Huastec Museum. 14k/9m farther along highway 70 you will come to the village of Tamuín. One mile past the village there is a bridge which crosses the Tamuín river. Signs indicate "San Vicente" and **El Tamuín.** You can take any bus going from Ciudad Valles to Tampico ("Oriente" is a good line) and get off at this same spot, or take the "Vencedor" line from Valles or Tamuín which passes the archaeological zone about once an hour. If you miss that bus you will have to walk to the ruins—and back! 5k/3m down this road there is a somewhat crude signboard indicating the ruins of **Tamuín**, once a very important *Huastec* and *Totonac* site. The entrance is through a gate opening with a cattle guard. The macadam road—800 meters—is a little rough in several places (daily, 7–6).

Tamuín (tahm-ween'), situated high above the river, was a cere-monial center which was thriving between 900 and 1500 A.D.

The main structure probably had three levels. The present plat-form is 14 meters long and 5 meters high, and is one of the few examples of a structure made with river stones. The walls were originally faced with stucco and painted. The small circles of stones in front of the platform indicate tombs. The long ceremonial altar still shows faint traces of a procession of priests and perhaps some warriors painted in red and yellow. (There are plans to have these restored to their original condition). The art has certain *Mixteca-Puebla* influences. Tombs were discovered under the circular areas. No extensive excavations had been made for many years, though R. Orellana worked at the site. The ceremonial altar was restored under the direction of the National Institute of Anthropology and history in 1978 by Noe Martínez González. In June of 1990 excavation work began under archaeologist José Maurilio Perea and will hopefully continue for some time. The major work has been the uncovering of the original stone face of the hill on which the structures were built, and its monumental staircase. A cistern for water storage and two other platforms have also been uncovered. Plans call for an on-site museum eventually.

From Tamuín to Tampico it is 112k/70m. If you do not want to go into Tampico, there is a detour toll road 9k/4.5m west of the city which connects with highway 180 to Tuxpan. See Route 1-A for directions to nearby Ciudad Madero and the museum there.

4-C: LAREDO/NUEVO LAREDO TO GUADALAJARA (1115K/693M, or 1003K/624M)

Starting at Nuevo Laredo, there are two routes to Guadalajara. The first is the same as Route 4-A as far as San Luis Potosí, where you can visit the museum. From here, highway 70/80 west will take you to Zapotlanejo to join highway 90 into Guadalajara. This route has some interesting towns and villages, but no archaeological sites. However, there is a surprising museum in Guadalupe (about 20k/12m south of Jalostitlán). It was created by two of Mexico's renowned archaeologists, Beatriz Barba and Román Piña Chan. It is in the annex of the city hall. There are two collections: one of reproductions of various cultures of Mexico, and the other of artifacts found in Jalisco, including offerings dredged up from Lake Chapala. There are buses from Nuevo Laredo to Guadalajara, also. See the beginning to Route 3 for details on travel, and for information on the geography and people of Pre-Columbian northern Mexico.

The second route uses highway 85 from the border at Nuevo Laredo to Monterrey (which can be bypassed 16k/10m before reaching the city by following the signs marked "Saltillo"). From the city highway 40 takes you to Saltillo. From here, highway 54 goes all the way to Guadalajara. The scenery varies from the rolling hills and desert plains in the north to the deep and sometimes awesome green valleys of the south. It offers only one archaeological site along the way, but it is one of the most impressive and interesting in Mexico and is known by two names: **Chicomoztoc** or La Quemada. Archaeologists are becoming more and more convinced that this site was the origin of many of the groups that later settled in the

Anáhuac or Mexico City valley. Its resemblance to some of the ruins of the southwest United States is striking. The ruins can be seen from the highway some 20k/12m south of the junction of highways 45/49 and 54 where you turn to go into Zacatecas. For the historical background on the *Chichimecs* and a description of this site, see Route 9-A.

Route 5: In and Around Mexico City

For a long time much of Mexico's archaeological activity centered logically in and around Mexico City, mainly because so much of the tangible evidence of its past was easily seen and frequently found. The huge metropolis of today covers an area which five centuries ago was a large lake situated in the heart of a vast highland plateau known as Anáhuac (An-nah'-wahk). The lake was called Texcoco (Tesh-ko'-ko) and only a small piece of it remains today near the city of the same name. Many of the city's suburbs, or important districts of Mexico City, like Tacubaya, Azcapotzalco and Coyoacán were actually little villages on the borders of the lake. It was in these little villages that the early settlers of the Anáhuac valley developed their civilization and culture, and where the Nahua-speaking peoples eventually banded to form the *Aztec* nation and empire. As the modern city expanded, machines and men unearthed all kinds of objects from earlier inhabitants. When the city built its subway system, hundred of artifacts were found beneath the former Aztec capital. All of this, together with the long-known Pre-Columbian structures, gave Mexican archaeology an impulse which continues to flourish. The traveler who goes nowhere except Mexico City can still learn a great deal about Mexico's past by visiting the numerous archaeological sites and museums.

MEXICO CITY'S EARLY HISTORY

Historians are not in complete agreement as to the origins and development of the *Aztec* culture and empire, but there is a general consensus that four major periods can be identified, with these approximate dates: a) 1169–1248, b) 1248–1376, c) 1376–1428, d) 1428–1521.

Around 1168, *Chichimec* nomadic groups began to move from the northwest into the central (Anáhuac) valley around the region of Lake Texcoco. Legend says that one of these groups came from a place called Aztlán, "the place of the storks," and so were called Aztecas, or the people from Aztlán. They had two chiefs, Mexitin and Tenoch. Those who followed the first were Mexicas, while the followers of the latter were Tenochas. Legend says that their god told

"Temple Mayor" in Mexico City.

them to settle wherever they would see an eagle with a serpent in its beak. At the present site of Chapultepec ("grasshopper hill") they saw the eagle sitting on a cactus, and the people settled there. At the beginning, however, after their arrival, they had been subjected by the Colhuas and Tepanecs who had formed a strong center at Azcapotzalco. The one thing which these groups had in common was their language—Nahuatl. A great deal of feuding went on between the groups around the lake, and in 1325 the Tenochas broke free and settled on an island in Lake Texcoco where Chapultepec was located.

The Mexica, meanwhile, were overpowering and incorporating into their own band the small lake villages. They succeeded in winning over the Tenochas, too, and moved into their city which had become known as **Tenochtitlán** and which was joined to the lake shore by four causeways. Some of the Tenochas moved to a nearby island, **Tlaltelolco**, but that, too, was taken over. By 1376 Tenochtitlán was a fairly strong city-state under Acampichtli. He is generally considered the first Aztec ruler.

From 1383 to 1420 Tenochtitlán grew under Acampichtli's two sons, Huitzilihuitl and Chimalpopoca. There was a diffusion of the Nahuatl language which facilitated later conquest and incorporation (like Latin with the Romans or Quechua with the Incas), and as assimilation of customs and culture which brought the Aztecs (as the combined Mexicas and Tenochas became known) to a higher degree of civilization than they had had before. At this same time, however, other cities like Azcapotzalco and Texcoco were also growing stronger.

In 1420 Acampichtli's third son, Itzcoatl, became ruler. Realizing the strength of the other city-states, he decided to form a league with them, thereby assuring equality while at the same time profiting from trade and cultural diffusion. Tenochtitlán grew strong, so that when Moctezuma I took over in 1440, things were ripe for the beginning of conquest. One by one the cities fell to the Aztecs: Ticomán, Tacuba, Coyocán, **Tenayuca**, and even the strong Azcapotzalco. When Moctezuma I died in 1469, most of central Mexico was dominated by the Aztecs who exacted tribute of all kinds from the subjected states and cities. His successor, Axayácatl (who was his cousin's son), in his fourteen-year reign conquered peoples as far away as the *Totonacs* on the gulf coast and the *Zapotecs* in the Oaxaca valley. His immediate successor, Tizoc, lived only three years, but Ahuitzotl (1486–1502) consolidated the empire and Aztec structures were built in places like **Teopanzolco, Tepozteco, Malinalco** and **Xochicalco**. Moctezuma II reigned for eighteen years over this formidable empire before he was suddenly faced with the invasion of it by the bearded white men armed in steel who kept him prisoner in his own palace. Killed, like Goliath, by a slung stone, Moctezuma II died in disgrace and was thought of as a traitor. His brother, Cuitlahuac, assumed the leadership and fought the Spaniards until he was killed. Cuautémoc, Ahuitzotl's son and the eleventh and last Aztec ruler, was captured after the fall of Tenochtitlán and held a prisoner for four years. Stories vary as to the place and manner of his death, but it is generally believed that he was killed somewhere in the Chiapas jungles while accompanying Cortés (by force) on his march to Honduras.

From the point of view of archaeology, three facets of the Aztec empire need a few words of explanation: the calendar, architecture and religious beliefs.

The Aztecs adopted the calendar of other cultures before them. The year was divided into twenty months of eighteen days (360), with a five-day period at the end which belonged to no month and was considered both special and dangerous. There was also a religious calendar of 260 days, and these two calendars operated somewhat independently. Every fifty-two years, they would coincide on day one. This was a tremendously terrifying and awesome time. All fires were extinguished and at the proper moment the chief priest would strike the flint to start the new fire. Should this fail, it would mean the end of the world. If successful, it would signify fifty-two more

Temple of the Wind Gods, Pino Suárez Metro station

years of life. This new lease on life was celebrated by constructing new temples, usually over existing ones. This explains the superimposition of pyramids at places like **Cholula** or **Teopanzolco**. Even elegant structures like the temple of Quetzalcoatl at **Teotihuacán** were covered over with new temple bases.

In general, Aztec architecture is forceful, massive and strong, but it often lacks the beauty and grace of that of other cultures. The Aztecs were imitators and copiers of the art of other cultures, as the Romans were of the Greeks. Yet, Tenochtitlán was so impressive to the Spaniards that one of the chroniclers wrote, "There is nothing like it in Spain!" The somewhat crude stone masonry was hidden beneath a surfacing of crushed limestone or adobe, in a kind of stucco fashion.

There were 78 buildings in the area which is central Mexico City today, 25 of them pyramids. The main plaza was over 300 meters on each side, and gates led to the causeways. In it were the main pyramid with shrines to the gods of war and rain on top of it, Moctezuma's palace, the skull rack, the temple to the sun, a temple to the minor gods and one to the night god. Axayácatl built his palace in Tacuba, and Moctezuma II had one on the Ixtapalapa road. There is a splendid model of the city in the Zócala metro station.

The feathered serpent, which appears in statues and paintings in various ways, was the main Aztec representation of Quetzalcoatl.

MEXICO CITY METRO SYSTEM

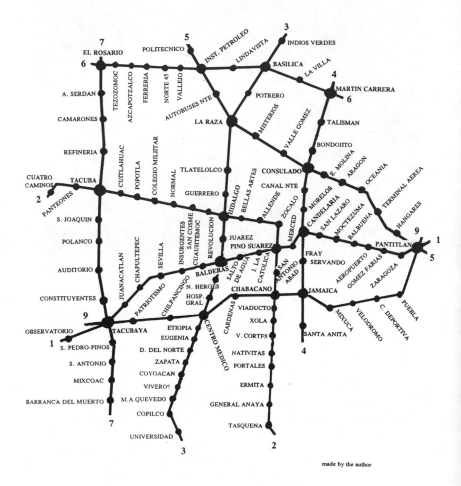

made by the author

This god came to represent different things, since he had been associated with different cultures. The basic legend to all of them was that he had been born of a virgin and taught the human race the arts and sciences and religion, and then left with a promise to return again some day from the east. He was said to have been bearded and of light skin. This legend-promise came to Moctezuma's mind when Cortés arrived on the gulf coast, and explains the Aztec ruler's hesitation to confront Cortés in battle which he could easily have done. It would be an honor to receive a god, and pointless to fight against him. By the time Moctezuma's doubts had been dispelled it

was too late, and the bearded men did take over, but in a way far different from that promised by Quetzalcoatl. It is also interesting to note that the Aztecs did not try to destroy the religions of their subjugated peoples but simply incorporated them into an Aztec pantheon, which is one reason why there were so many temple pyramids.

Now, some directives on how to visit many of the places mentioned.

5-A: IN THE CITY ITSELF

A1: The National Museum of History and Anthropology (Tue–Sat, 9–7; Sun, 10–6; Adm. except Sun), located a short distance off of Reforma across from the zoo in Chapultepec park, is one of the finest museums in the world, both architecturally and archaeologically speaking. Take line 7 of the Metro to the stop marked "Auditorio." You will have about a ten-minute walk east on Reforma to the entrance. Buses numbers 55 or 76 marked "Auditorio" going west on Reforma will leave you practically at the entrance. You will need several hours to go through the museum thoroughly. Try to do so on a weekday (the museum is closed on Mondays) because hundreds of visitors are there on weekends. All of the major Mexican Pre-Columbian cultures are represented, and there is a magnificent scale model of **Tenochtitlán**. The second floor of the museum is devoted mainly to ethnology, with reproductions of housing, tools, utensils, artifacts, clothing etc. of the various cultures and regions of Mexico. Don't miss the reconstruction of the famous **Bonampak** temple in one of the museum gardens. The huge monolithic statue in front of the museum is a representation of Tlaloc, the god of rain. Sculpted around 900 A.D., the statue is 24½ ft. high and weighs 167 tons. It was moved here in 1964 from Coatlinchán, not far from **Texcotzingo**. If you wonder about the efficacy of the gods, consider this: the day it was moved there was a tremendous downpour, ending one of Mexico City's longest droughts!

A2: One block from the main plaza (popularly called the Zócalo— so'-kah-lo) on the corner of Guatemala and Argentina streets across from the back side of the cathedral, excavations from 1978 through 1988 uncovered the base of the original main temple of Tenochtitlán and other samples of Aztec masonry, all kinds of artifacts (27,000 of them!) as well as some fine sculptures like the beautiful Coyolxauhqui stone (12 tons) and statues of Huitzilopochtli and Tlaloc whose temples stood on top of the pyramid. Visitors may walk through these ruins from 10 to 5, Tuesday through Sunday (Adm.). There is also a fine museum here with some superb sculptures found at the site. These ruins are just a block away from the Zócalo metro stop.

A3: Tlaltelolco (tlah-tay-lowl'-ko) was the central market place of the Aztec capital and the trading center for much of early Mexico. Today it is known as the Plaza of the Three Cultures, indicated on city maps in the northeast sector. There is a metro stop of the same name about 5 blocks west of the ruins. City buses (brown/yellow 100) going east on Reforma will take you also within a few blocks (south) of this plaza.

The site was originally an island in Lake Texcoco, and was settled in 1337 by Tenochas who were unhappy with things at nearby **Tenochtitlán**. However, the *Aztec* ruler Axayácatl absorbed the island into his expanding kingdom in 1473 and joined it to Tenochtitlán with a causeway. Eventually it became the "tanguis" or central market place of the Aztec capital, and as many as 25,000 buyers and sellers milled through it daily. A special police group maintained order, inspected measurements and merchandise, and checked on prices which were government regulated and subject to federal tax (using today's terminology). Overlooking this vast commercial complex was a huge pyramid, second only in size to the great Teocalli of Tenochtitlán. The Spaniards and Indian allies captured before the "noche triste" were sacrificed here. The last battle against the Spaniards was fought here on August 13, 1521. Cortés claimed that the center was twice the size of Salamanca. The ruins were discovered in 1944–48 in the construction of the present Plaza of the Three Cultures (Pre-Columbian market, colonial church and modern Ministry of Foreign Affairs). E. Mengin has edited the *Annals* of Tlaltelolco.

A4: The Pino Suárez Metro station on lines 1 and 2 has an altar to Ehécatl, the wind god, which was found while excavations were being

San Pedro de Los Pinos

made for the subway. There are also some artifacts on display in the station.

A5: San Pedro de los Pinos, which underwent restorations during 1990, is right next to the Outer Loop (Periférico) on Calle Pirámide, between Calles 20 and 22, one block north of Avenida San Antonio, and three west of Avenida Revolución. From the highway, use the San Antonio exit and turn back east. From in town, take Insurgentes Sur to San Antonio, turn right and go to one block from the Outer Loop. Turn right on Pirámide. Metro station "San Antonio" (*not* "San Pedro de los Pinos!") is a five-minute walk; go west on San Antonio toward the Outer Loop and north to Calle 20.

This well-preserved site, open to the public since 1942, is often overlooked. It was discovered in 1912 and restored in 1915 by E. Noguera. The several structures have been identified as *Toltec* architecture and are thought to have been the palace complex of the Toltec king Mixcoac, or Mixcohuatl, at the time the Toltecs were in this region early in the tenth century.

5-B: OUTLYING BUT CLOSE ARCHAEOLOGICAL AREAS

B1—To the south: a) The unique Diego Rivera Anahuacalli Museum has a fabulous collection of Pre-Columbian pieces. It is situated about two kilometers south of Miguel Angel Quevedo street, and west of División del Norte street on Calle Museo 150. City buses or streetcars

Recently discovered ruins of Acozac near Mexico City

stop just a couple of blocks away. (Tue–Sun, 10–2, 3–5). There is no admission charge.

b) Copilco has interesting Pre-Christian era burial caves, and a small museum. Follow Av. Universidad south. A block after you cross Miguel Angel Quevedo take Oxtopulco (right) to Callejón Palma. Go left to Capilla, and left again to Clavel. One more left and the site and museum are at the end of this street. You can follow the same directions if you get off at Metro stop "Miguel Angel Quevedo" on line 3 (*not* "Copilco"). Buses 17 and 7A on Insurgentes Sur will get you within easy walking distance (take Progreso street to Capilla, then right to Clavel).

Copilco (ko-peel'-ko: Tue–Sun, 9–5, Adm.) means "the place of the diadem." This is one of the early sites of central Mexico and thrived between 1200 and 700 B.C. Some time around the latter date, Lake Texcoco flooded, forcing the inhabitants to leave the area. Some time after this, the volcano Xitle, 16k/10m away, erupted, burying the whole area under some 7 meters of lava. The first excavation of the site was made in 1917, by M. Gamio. Subsequent digging revealed underground caves used for burials. It is these that may be visited today. The excavations revealed bones and pottery from 1500 B.C. (90% of the pottery utilitarian), clay images, deerhorn and shell ornaments, stone tools, spiral basketwork and obsidian blades. The small museum at the site contains a number of these objects.

c) Cuicuilco (kwee-kwill'-ko: Tue–Sun, 10–5; Adm. except Sun) may be the oldest pyramid in the Americas. It is certainly one of the earliest. There is a small museum here also. Follow Insurgentes Sur past the Ciudad Universitaria to the Outer Loop (Periférico). Right after you go under this expressway there will be a small road to the left. This will take you to the site. (You will have passed the road to **Copilco** on the way). The city bus to Tlalpan (number 17) passes the site.

Meaning "among varied colors," the site was first excavated by M. Gamio and B. Cummings in 1922. Many archaeologists have since worked here, including E. Noguera, H. Moedano and R. Heizer. Plans for the 1960 Olympic games focused attention on the area, and archaeological salvage work began in May, 1967, under the direction of P. Salazar Ortegón and A. Cuevas. More work began in 1989 and is still going on. Efforts are being made to uncover a platform structure to the east of the main pyramid.

Ticoman people settled here around 900 B.C. and the population was increased by refugees from **Copilco**. Originally this was an agricultural community which also had stonecutters, weavers, potters and masons. They built what may be the oldest manmade structure in the Anáhuac valley. They had an organized religion, and constructed a pyramid of four terraces, circular in shape, made of rock walls filled with earth and faced with volcanic rock. This was done between 300 and 200 B.C. The pyramid was rebuilt twice, so that the final structure is nearly 114 meters in diameter, and 19 meters high. There was a circular temple on top with an adobe altar painted red. The stairway is on the east side. In the vicinity of the pyramid other shrines were built, mainly altars on leveled platforms. The houses were grass huts. The dead were buried with offerings under the floor of the house, in extended or flexed positions. 23 skeletons were found in 1967, some of them showing cranial deformation. The pyramid temple was dedicated to Huehueteotl, the old fire god, whose cult and presence became a reality when nearby Xitle volcano erupted (opinions differ as to exactly when, but most believe in the early years of the Christian era) and buried the lower third of the structure and all those around it with lava, killing all life in the area and forcing the people to find a new home.

d) Xochimilco was once an important agricultural producing area for the *Aztec* capital. Today it is an over-frequented tourist spot full of people anxious to embark in the flower-filled boats to ride up and down the canals. These very canals, however, have made a museum possible. One way to get to it is to take the Outer Loop to the Xochimilco road, and follow it south heading for Santa Cruz Acalpixcan. On Tenochtitlán street you will find the Xochimilco Archaeological Museum (Tue–Sun, 9–5;

Little known Pre-Columbian site of Tlapacoya

Adm.) where some 10,000 objects found in the surrounding waters have been gathered. 2,300 of them are on display in two rooms. This place can also be reached by vans of Lines A and B which can be found on the north side of the south bus terminal. Unless you don't mind traffic-choked streets, avoid Xochimilco on Sundays when hordes of Mexicans and tourists descend on it.

B2—to the east: For all of the sites to the east of Mexico City, you will need to use the free highway 150/190 (it has two numbers until it reaches Puebla; the toll road is 150D). There are two main ways to reach this highway. One is to take Ignacio Zaragoza street near the expressway to the airport and follow it all the way to where it meets highway 150/190 at Los Reyes. The other way is to take a street at the south end of town (it changes names from José Rico to Popocatépetl to Ermita Ixtapalapa to Avenida del Molino) and go east toward highway 150/190. You will pass the Cerro de la Estrella (Hill of the Star). This was the *Toltec* center and an extremely important site in *Aztec* times since it was on this hill that the new fire was struck every 52 years. Small caves in the hill were used as ritual centers and in colonial times chapels were built around them to "Christianize" them. There are ruins of a temple on top of the hill, and even today people occasionally find small figurines and pieces of broken pottery. There is a museum here featuring funerary offerings, musical instruments and weapons.

a) Tlapacoya (tlah-pah-ko'-yah) is a little-known but fascinating Pre-Columbian site. Take the free highway 190/150 past the junction with highway 136 north to k 28 (you will go through the town of Ayotla about halfway). When you reach a big yellow walkway over the highway turn right onto the paved road. It turns into a dirt road about halfway to the village. At the church turn left on a narrow, bumpy dirt road for a block and then uphill (right) to the cemetery. A few paces up the hill to the right is the entrance (daily, 10–5).

Centuries ago this site was an island in Lake Texcoco. People may have lived on it as long as 20,000 years ago. Between 800 and 200 B.C. it was a small agricultural village which came under certain *Olmec* influences (a roller stamp bearing three Olmec glyphs was found here). These people built a large earth platform, attached to the central hill, faced it with rocks, and put a small temple on top. Tlapacoya became one of the first religious centers, just about the time that Cuicuilco was being formed. With time, the platform was enlarged with six tiers, all faced with stone. A side stairway was added to each new temple, and the hill itself was faced with a retaining wall. The overall effect gives the impression of the super imposition of a number of small platforms, producing thirteen "stories."

In the last addition, three tombs were made and covered with basalt monolithic slabs. The visitor can see the tombs at the top of the present structure. According to the official reports, what is visible is only one-third of the whole massive structure! At the beginning of the Christian era, Tlapacoya began to lose importance due to the rise of **Teotihuacán** and perhaps other centers. It continued down into *Aztec* times, however, during which it became a weaving center. Pottery found ranges from simple incised black ware to polished red ware with ornamental supports in animal forms. Also found were figurines, jade beads, spiral-weave baskets, obsidian knives, bone needles, etched seashells and other types of tools and ornaments. Cranial deformation and filing of teeth were practiced by these people. Studies at this site were made in 1956 by B. Barba and R. Piña Chan.

b) Very close by is **Acozac** (ah-ko-sock') best known as a golf course, but there are excellent ruins on the hill overlooking it and the new subdivision which has developed there. Follow the free highway 150/190 to **Tlapacoya** as indicated above. About two kilometers farther on, a long, tree-lined road to the left leads into the new subdivision with a paved road to the top of a nearby hill. You will have to pass the clubhouse and a guard gate on your way up. There is a maze of blacktop roads. Keep generally to the left as you ascend. If you miss the site, drive

Huexotia ruins just off the road.

to the top of the hill and look down. You'll see both the site and the road to it (daily, 9–5).

Acozac in Nahua means "in the yellow water." These ruins are of fairly recent discovery. Work began in 1970, led by R. Piña Chan. Situated on the hill, this site probably overlooked Lake Texcoco in early times. Four structures are standing: a stepped pyramid dedicated to Ehécatl (the wind god), a sector of living quarters, and two stone platform structures. 22 mounds covering structures dot the site, one most certainly part of a ball court. The masonry is of an early kind. The partial room structures still have some of the original flooring in them. Farther down below, surrounded by houses, there is a small stepped pyramid and a platform structure with a wide frontal staircase, perhaps the palace complex of some priest or nobleman. The abundance and types of pottery sherds found indicate that there was a long occupation which culminated in incorporation into the *Aztec* empire. A unique site, it was probably one of the many hilltop ceremonial centers.

c) Huexotla (way-showt'-lah) is another of the early villages of the Anáhuac valley. Take the free highway 190 east to the junction with highway 136. Take 136 north about 20k/12.5m to the road (right) which leads to the site (5k). Drive to the end of the dirt road along the immense defense wall of the city. From here you must walk a dirt path along a field for about 50 yards. A cyclone fence surrounds the area, and the gate is not always open.

This "place of willows" was not far from the shores of the original Lake Texcoco, and was in fact a subject city-state of Texcoco. It was built by Ixtlixóchitl, the father of the famous poet-philosopher-king Nezahualcóyotl who ruled from 1427 to 1470 A.D. R. García Granados worked here in 1952–53. The outstanding feature is the remaining fragment of the impressive wall, nearly 5 meters high and 62 meters long. A round pyramid to the wind god, with a spiral staircase, itself a symbol of the wind, is partially excavated. A large platform area with smaller platforms on it resembles **Tlaltelolco** and may have been the same kind of thing—a market place. Little else has been excavated, though there are mounds in the vicinity. Many of the houses around are built on the foundations of Pre-Columbian structures, or have used stone from them.

d) Four kilometers north of **Huexotla** you come to the city of Texcoco. Go into town on B. Juárez street. Watch for Abasolo street (right). You will have to go one more block, turn east and go to the end of the street and turn back right onto Abasolo, which is one way west. Near the end of the street you will see the **Los Melones** archaeological site (daily, 9–12; 3–5).

e) Texcotzingo (tesh-coat-sing'-go) popularly known as the Baths of Nezahuacóyotl requires a fairly good climb to the top of a hill. If that thought doesn't discourage you, then there are two ways to get to the site. One is to take the free highway 150/190 east to the junction with highway 136 and follow it north to Texcoco and east 3k to Molino de Flores Park. (This takes you past **Huexotla** above). Follow the park road uphill, always taking the left branch at any fork in the road, until you reach the parking area. You climb from there. The other route is to take Insurgentes Norte from town to highway 85, follow the free road to Tepexpan (see 5-C1 for a note on the museum here) and turn south until you meet highway 136 going east at Texcoco (see "d" above for the museum here).

Texcotzingo means "laughing hill." Nezahualcóyotl built a palace between 1455 and 1467 and had "baths" hewn from the rock and provided with aqueducts 27 kilometers long. The statues carved here were among the best of pre-Aztec Mexico. The palace had such things as conference rooms, a treasury, a court room and arsenal. The site has been studied by W. Krickeberg (1949) and H. B. Nicholson (1959). On a clear day there is a fine view from this hill.

B3—TO THE NORTH:

a) **Tenayuca** (tay-nah-you'kah: Tue–Sun, 10–5, Adm) is one of the few *Aztec* pyramids still standing. Follow either Calzada Vallejo or Av. de los Cien Metros in the northwest sector of town about 7k/4m to where it forks with the road going into Progreso Nacional subdivision. Take the road into the subdivision and the pyramid is 500 meters down the road and a bit east. Trolleybuses marked "Tenayuca" pass the north terminal. At the "Politécnico" Metro station (line 5), go out the west (PTE) exit. There are three lanes of buses; all go to or past Tenayuca. The white vans in the third lane cost a little more but are faster. Another option is from the "Indios Verdes" Metro station (last on line 3). Exits C and D take you to buses that go to Tenayuca.

Tenayuca means "walled city." The site was first excavated between 1925 and 1928, and again in 1935 by A. Caso and E. Noguera. It was probably begun in 1224 A.D. by Xólotl, leader of the Acolhuas, a *Chichimec* group. This is one of the finest examples of the superimposition of pyramids. The first structure was 31 × 12 meters and 8 meters high. It is on an exact east-west axis when the sun is at its zenith. Succeeding constructions were made in 1299, 1351, 1403, 1455 and 1507, or every 52 years. The last three are in *Aztec* style. The final structure covers 68 × 76 meters and is 17 meters high. There are 70 steps to the top. The 138 snakes in stone around the base represent Quetzalcoatl. Those on the south and east sides were painted blue, and those on the north, black. There was an altar of skulls, which is now in the Mexico City museum. The crests on the snakes near the east side platform are symbolic of the equinoxes and solstices. The overall construction is a fairly good idea of what the major temple at **Tenochtitlán** looked like, but on a smaller scale.

b) **Santa Cecilia** (sahn'-tah say-seal'yah), also called Acatitlán, is an archaeological gem, a reconstructed temple to the rain god. Follow the route to **Tenayuca** above and continue on another kilometer or so to this new subdivision. The temple is next to the church in a little plaza. Enter through the museum on the southwest corner (8–5; Adm.).

This site probably dates from the same time as **Tenayuca**. The four-tiered temple platform may originally have had two small temples on top, but one of them was certainly dedicated to the rain god, which the present reconstruction is meant to represent. The restoration gives a good idea of what such structures looked like, and from that point of view alone it is worth visiting.

In the northern part of the Federal District are the districts of Arbolillo, Ticomán and Zacatenco, all early farming settlements (1500–800 B.C.) where many earthen figurines have been found. This whole area is now urbanized. Two nearby municipalities, both somewhat northeast, have museums in their Casa de la Cultura. The one in Nezahualcoyòtol is at 4a Avenida and Virgen de Lourdes. It has a few pieces, mural-size photos of various sites and objects from the Mexico Valley in general. In Ecatepec, on Plaza Juárez 1, the focus is on *Mexica* art with some sculptures and a portrayal of the ball game. Ecatepec and Tepexpan can be visited (see 5-C1 for details) and combined with **Texcotzingo** (5-B2, e).

There are no major archaeological sites immediately west of Mexico City that can be visited. However, it is worth noting that hundreds of clay figurines have been found at **Tlatilco**, an important farming community around 800 B.C. Tlatilco gave birth to **Copilco** and other settlements. It is important not only as a focal point for the rise of culture and civilization in central Mexico, but also because evidence of the extensive spread of the *Olmec* culture has been found here in the form of figurines, a roller stamp and an axe handle. The bottle-shaped burial chambers have been found all around this area. M. Covarrubias worked here in 1943 and R. Piña Chan in 1952 and 1960. The museum in Mexico City contains an exact replica, complete with skeletons and grave offerings, of a Tlatilco burial, and the Anahuacalli museum also has numerous pieces. Most of present-day Tlatilco is a sprawling and somewhat depressing slum area.

5-C: ARCHAEOLOGICAL DAYTRIPS FROM MEXICO CITY

There are a number of archaeological areas you can visit while keeping Mexico City as your "base camp." Most of those to be mentioned are found along one of the regular travel routes, and you will find descriptions and details by looking for the name of the site in the Index. Remember that one day a week you can't use your car (see p. 16).

C1) Teotihuacán (tay-oh-tee-wah-kahn') is one of the most important Pre-Columbian centers anywhere in the Americas. It lies 48k/30m northeast of Mexico City. There are a number of tourist and travel agencies which offer trips daily, including the "light and sound" show during the "dry" months. Autobuses San Juan Teotihuacán (counter at the far west end of the north bus terminal) leave about every half hour. There are also buses from the "Indios Verdes" Metro station, exits A and B. If you are driving, take Insurgentes Norte to highway 85. Both the toll road and the free road will take you to San Juan de Teotihuacán and the archaeological zone (daily, 8–6; 8–11 for "light and sound shows;" Adm.). The free road goes through some interesting towns, especially Acolmán. Along the way you can go into Ecatepec. As you enter on Av. Insurgentes, you will see a high hill to your right. If you are feeling especially energetic and wanting to do something different, a road will take you to the base of the hill. A half-hour climb will bring you to a cave which still has some art work in it and was dedicated to the wind god. If you continue on Insurgentes you will cross Calle Juárez. Turn right, and next to the church is the Casa de la Cultura which has a museum (Mon–Fri, 9–5). On the other side of the

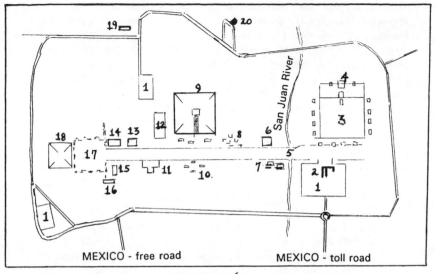

MEXICO - free road   MEXICO - toll road

TEOTIHUACÁN

1. parking area
2. museum/main entrance (probably the original market)
3. the citadel
4. temple of Quetzalcoatl
5. avenue of the dead
6. temple of Tlaloc (site of the 1917 excavations)
7. superimposed structures
8. Viking group
9. pyramid of the sun
10. patio of the 4 little temples
11. temple of the columns
12. palace
13. temple of the jaguar
14. temple of the frescos
15. temple of the butterfly
16. palace of the jaguars
17. plaza of the moon
18. pyramid of the moon
19. tepantitla (famous mural)
20. "cave" restaurant

church is the tomb of José M. Morelos, one of the great independence heroes of Mexico.

From Ecatepec there is a toll road (marked "Pirámides") to Teotihuacán. If you take this road, you can turn off at the road to Tepexpan, just before the toll gates. Right there (to the left) there is an entrance to a fence enclosed area which has the Prehistory Museum of Tepexpan (Tue–Sun, 10–5). There is a replica of the grave found here with one of the oldest known skeletons—a man who died trying to kill a mammoth 13,000 years ago, and some mammoth bones. Both were found in 1947. If you stayed on the free road from Ecatepec which goes into Tepexpan, you will have to go out to the west end of town (look for signs to the "Pirámides" toll road) to come to the museum area.

You will need a few hours at **Teotihuacán** in order to see everything. If you get hungry, visit the Grotto Restaurant for a totally different but very pleasant atmosphere and experience.

It would probably be safe to say that no other archaeological site in the Americas has been so visited, studied, researched or worked at as this place "where the gods dwell." Among the important investigations and contributions to the knowledge of this center are those of L. Bartres (1905–1910), M. Gamio (1917–1922), S. Linné (1932–1935) and P. Armillas (1942–1945). More recent work includes the mapping of the whole valley by J. Parsons, the mapping of the city itself by R. Millon, and the excavation and restoration of building 40-A in the east plaza complex (1982). From its humble beginnings this city grew to be the greatest Pre-Columbian center in the New World and its influence, particularly throughout Mesoamerica, was enormous.

As early as 1000 B.C. people were settling in the valley along the river. By 500 B.C. there were agricultural groups which received cultural influences from the *Olmecs*. At the beginning of the Christian era, some 14,000 inhabitants lived in the valley, and had banded together into a kind of single society. Their culture began to develop around 100 A.D. and grew through two building periods, three ceramic phases and five figurine styles. One of the earliest structures was the majestic pyramid of the sun (see map site, 9) which occupied 10,000 people for twenty years. The core of this is 1,300,000 cubic yards of rubble and rocks which was afterwards faced with stone, stuccoed and painted. On the 40-meter base at the top stood a temple made of wood and reeds. The structure measures 224 meters at the base and is 60 meters high. It is so perfectly aligned that its east-west axis coincides exactly with the horizon point of the setting sun after it has passed its zenith. The nearby pyramid of the moon (18) may be a little older. It is 150 × 120 meters at the base, and 42 meters high. Around these imposing religious structures the city was divided into sections, each devoted to a special group by class or trade, and houses were built for clan groups. Sometimes they were patios with fifty or sixty rooms around them, with an altar in each complex. Other areas had more individual-type houses, probably for nobles, overseers, etc. In 1987 and 1989 excavations in the Oaxaca sector (called Tlaclotlacán) revealed Zapotaec characteristics in the architecture and ceramics.

By 300 A.D. the city covered 20 square kilometers, and had 100,000 inhabitants. The main buildings were laid out in a north-south direction on both sides of an avenue (5) a little over a kilometer and a half long and 55 meters wide. The *Aztecs* mistakenly called this the "avenue of the dead" because they found burials under some of the structures. By 500 A.D. the metropolis was thriving and was exporting its products, especially obsidian objects, to centers hundreds of kilometers away. There was a lively trade with the early *Maya* centers for quetzal feathers, jade, cotton, copal, seashells and rubber. Teotihuacán art work can still be seen in the Temple of Agriculture and the Tepantitla palace (19), and the Temple of the Frescoes (14). It is forceful and realistic, and some of it was done in "mass production" in molds. Death masks in jade, alabaster and other stone became a trademark. Religious art found some of its first expression. The gods of Teotihuacán were exported along with the art and commercial goods so that there was scarcely any center which did not feel the impact of this powerful city in some form or another. It is said that these people were the first tortilla makers, and that art, too, spread far and wide!

By 600 A.D. there were around 200,000 people in the city and 2,600 structures. Society was organized into castes: the priests and rulers, the merchants, the artists, the peasants and the servants and slaves. Nearby areas became incorporated into this city-state which only **Cholula** began to rival about this same time. Then, about 650 A.D., disaster struck. This great city had never built fortifications or defenses; it had never had any need to. Marauding tribes from the north began to attack. The city was burned and looted, perhaps in successive stages. The people began to flee and settled in Cholula or in other parts farther south and east. By 750 the great city was all but totally dead. Some people stayed on, because when the *Toltecs* began to build their cities, they got artisans from among those still in this area. Some things about Teotihuacán indicate that the Toltecs may have settled there, too. The Aztecs definitely did take over this center, and claimed that the Fifth Sun was born there when Nanahuatzin threw himself into a sacrificial fire. They added some new structures, particularly to their own gods, in the section known as "the citadel" (3) covering over the magnificent sculpture of the temple to Quetzalcoatl (4), also called the Temple of the Frog, associated with the rain (the alternate stone sculptures with those of the feathered snake represent Tlaloc, the rain god). The city revived somewhat, but it never regained its former splendor.

C2) Tula, the *Toltec* capital, is 96k/60m northwest of Mexico City on Route 4-A. Buses marked "Valle de Mezquital" leave for Tula from the far west end of the north terminal every 15 minutes. It's about a 20-minute walk to the ruins from town.

C3) Calixtlahuaca is 8k/5m north of Toluca, which is 64k/40m west of Mexico City. See Route 8-B. There is also a museum in Toluca. Buses leave from the west terminal.

C4) Highway 55 south from Toluca will enable you to see two intriguing sites. The first, **Teotenango**, is on a hilltop overlooking the town of Tenango, 25k/16m from Toluca. The bus line "Tres Estrellas del Centro" comes here from Mexico City's west terminal.

Teotenango (tay-oh-tay-nahn'-go: Tue–Sun, 9–5; Adm) means "divine wall," and this was a ceremonial center for both **Malinalco** and

Calixtlahuaca. It covered some 21 square kilometers and was surrounded on three sides by a double wall 6 meters high. The site was originally established by the Matlazincas perhaps as early as 2000 B.C. Refugees from **Teotihuacán** (650 A.D.) brought advanced knowledge with them and the city flourished. It was conquered by the *Aztecs* during the reign of Axayácatl which began in 1474, and was given to the young Moctezuma as a fief. This fascinating center went ignored for years, and only in 1971 was restoration begun. Work has moved rapidly and many structures have already been completed. The ball court, bath house and serpent base building are most notable. Among other interesting things found was a sculpture of a monster eating the sun—a depiction of the solar eclipse of 1477. A museum named for the Mexican archaeologist Román Piña Chan has samples of pottery, sculpture, weapons and tools found during the excavations.

24k/15m farther on is the town of Tenancingo. From here a somewhat winding road (left) will take you to **Malinalco** which some say means "a turn in the road." Others prefer "a twisted reed," from the word "malinalli."

Malinalco (mah-lee-nahl'-ko: 10–4:30; Adm.) was discovered by J. García Payón in 1936, and he worked there in 1956–57. From 1987–1989 restoration and preservation work was done. This area was settled by people related to the Matlazincas (see **Calixtlahuaca**) and who were later dominated by the Acolhuas from the Anáhuac valley. The *Aztec* ruler Axayácatl conquered the site in 1469 A.D. The main archaeological monument, however, dates from 1501. It is a religious sanctuary carved out of the rock at the top of the hill known as Cerro de los Idolos (Hill of Idols). It is a semicircular "temple" about 4 meters deep. The entrance is carved to resemble a serpent's jaws, the earth monster, and carvings of jaguars flank the stairway. One historian says that the temple was dedicated to the sun god, and the jaguars and eagle (carved on the temple floor) are symbols of the warrior knights who were sworn to fight against evil, represented by the earth monster-like entrance. (The "structure" is also referred to as the Temple of the Eagle and Jaguars). It was here that Aztec youths were initiated into these groups. Nearby there are some large rooms, also carved out of the rock. In the area known as Group III, murals depict a procession of soldiers with shields and spears. This may have been the Tzinacalli, the place for death rites. The multi-level terraces were undoubtedly meant for various types of structures. The war theme is not surprising since it was the Aztec ruler Ahuitzotl who ordered the making of this sanctuary site. Stonecutters from **Tenochtitlán** were employed to work here, but the cutting was never completed, possibly because Ahuitzotl died the following year.

Both of the above sites can also be reached from Cuernavaca by buses to Tenancingo or Tenango. The one to Malinalco starts in Chalma, so a transfer is necessary.

C5) There are three sites to the south which are a good daytrip (if you start early enough!). The first, **Teopanzolco** lies within the city limits of Cuernavaca (Route 7). 18k/11m east of Cuernavaca the cliff-top pyramid of **Tepozteco** overlooks the city of Tepotzlán (Route 6-A4). And 34k/21m south and west of Cuernavaca lies a site well worth the trip if you have the time: **Xochicalco** (Route 7).

The road to Xochicalco continues west to Miacatlán and then Mazatepec (**Coatetelco** is just a short distance from here; see Route 7) and on to Cacahuamilpa and the famous cave there—a splendor of stalactites and stalagmites if you want to add some speleology to your archaeology. The road then joins highway 55 where you can turn north and visit the sites mentioned in 4) above. And when you get to Toluca if time permits you can visit **Calixtlahuaca** (see Route 8-B). You can complete this "circle trip" by returning to Mexico City from Toluca on highway 15 or 134. The circuit is 312k/-195m. Realistically, however, counting the time needed to visit the sites, the trip would need two days unless only certain sites are selected.

C6) Cholula, among Mexico's most important sites, is 120k/75m east of Mexico City, near Puebla (see Route 6-A1). The toll road is excellent. However, it would be possible to begin by using the free highway 150/190 to stop at **Tlapacoya** and **Acozac** (see 5-B2, "a" and "b") and you can join the toll road farther on. There is frequent bus service to Puebla from the east bus terminal (the "San Lázaro" station on metro line 1). From Puebla buses leave for Cholula from 8 poniente, between 7 and 9 norte.

If you leave early enough another "circle trip" is possible. Take highway 119 north from Puebla to where it meets highway 117. Turn west and go 8k/5m to reach **Tizatlán** (see Route 6-A1 for details). Return to 119 and go north to highway 136. Turn west. 50k/31m farther on you will come to the road to Calpulapan. Go north toward San Mateo and 1.5k farther on you will come to the site of **Tecoaque** (not mentioned in any other route).

Tecoaque (tay-ko-ah'-kay) was a ceremonial center surrounded by clusters of houses. In the plaza there is the circular base of a temple to the wind god, with an altar in front. There are some sunken patios with rooms around them, presumably quarters for the priests. The system of drainage canals is cleverly done. This was a relatively late settlement (1300–1500 A.D.). R. Piña Chan has done some archaeological work here.

Continuing west, as you near Texcoco you will pass the Molino de Flores Park, and the entrance to **Texcotzingo** (see 5-B2, "e"). From Texcoco you can take highway 136 south (back to 190 where you started) and visit **Huexotla** (see 5-B2, "c"). This round trip is 272k/170m.

Route 6: The Pan-American Highway and Alternatives East and South from Mexico City

Highway 190, part of the original Pan American highway, is one of Mexico's longest and most scenic routes. It goes from Mexico City all the way to the Mexico-Guatelmala border (1,312k/815m). Well over half of it is through rugged and sometimes spectacular mountain country. The stretch between Tehuantepec and Tuxtla Gutiérrez is typical tropical country. Today there are several alternate routes to the Pan American highway, though highway 190 is still the main artery from Puebla to Tehuantepec. The newer routes are frequently faster, sometimes more scenic, and offer alternate areas of archaeological interest. The Puebla and Oaxaca regions are of major archaeological importance. It should be noted that highway 190 is also 150 as far as Puebla.

6-A: MEXICO CITY TO OAXACA (510K/318M; 560K/351M).

There are four possible routes from Mexico City to Oaxaca: 1) via Puebla, 2) via Puebla-Tehuacán, 3) via Cuautla and 4) via Cuernavaca-Cuautla. The first three will take you past **Tlapacoya** and **Acozac** described in Route 5-B2 which also explains how to get to highway 190. Oaxaca and the important archaeological zones along highway 190 south are described in Route 6-B.

A1—VIA PUEBLA (534K/332M)

Puebla can be reached by the free highway 190/150 or the toll road, 150D. Several bus companies leave Mexico City's east terminal for Puebla. If you are really in a hurry, "Flecha Roja" has a departure every five minutes. The free road offers several archaeological possibilities. The first two, **Tlapacoya** and **Acozac** are found in Route 5-B2, a and b. A detour from 150 at 91k/56m will take you to two little-known sites, the first of them a relatively recent and exciting discovery. When you get to San Martín Texmelucan, watch for signs to Nativitas and **Cacaxtla**. 3k before you reach Nativitas, a road left goes to San Miguel del Milagro. The museum here houses the artifacts from **Cacaxtla** which is one k north-

103

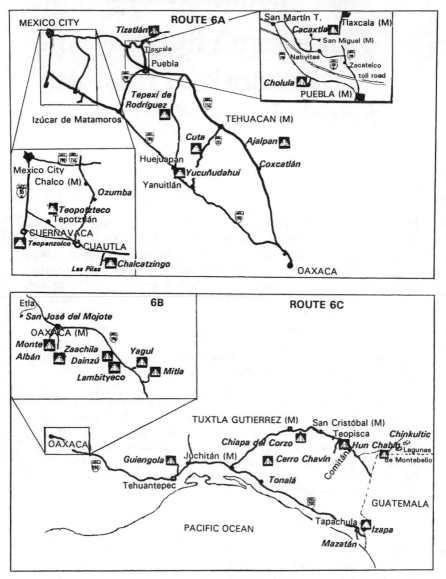

west and describes its famous wall paintings. From the parking area you will have to walk about 500 meters.

The area around Cacaxtla (kah-kasht'-lah) was inhabited very early by a group with *Olmec* characteristics. They built platforms of various levels on which they placed their structures. The three surrounding hills were inhabited and defended by moats and thick walls which enclosed an area of 32,000 square meters. At first this was a ceremonial site visited by pilgrims from surrounding villages. Attacked by the warriors from **Cholula** and Huejotzingo, the center was walled and strongly fortified. The structures at the north platform and the pillared portico with the now famous "Battle Mural" were probably done around 700 A.D. The painted walls are done in panels 1.80 × 2.50 meters. The frescoes in red, blue, black and ocre contain **Teotihuacán** elements like serpents, flowers and marine animals. The figures in jaguar and bird costumes reflect more the later groups. Between 800 and 1200 the *Chochopolocas, Mixtecs*, and *Nahuas* also left vestiges of their different styles of architecture. The oldest building found so far, Building E, clearly shows a *Maya* influence. The door jambs represent huge plants of corn, and a personage depicted on one of the pillars wears typical Mayan dress and is surrounded by corn. One figure is very similar to the Maya God-B.

The center has a great plaza, three pyramids and several platforms. Although the site was mentioned by some of the early Spanish chroniclers who considered it a fortress, it was not discovered until 1975 when illegal treasure hunters accidentally exposed the painted wall. Work has been going on here ever since, mainly under Angel García and archaeologists of the I.N.A.H. In May of 1991 some new paintings were discovered, and it becomes more and more evident that this was a major center on the coast-to-highland road.

Continue on to Tlaxcala where there is a very fine museum in the ex-Franciscan convent on a hill at the south end of the Xicoténcatl plaza on Morelos and Independencia streets. From the city the easiest way to get to the ancient Tlaxcalan capital is to take any street north to Julián Carrillo. Follow this west (it becomes Zahuapan) to highway 117. Turn right toward Apizaco and 3k/1.5m farther on you come to the town of Tizatlán. A path up the hill from the highway takes you to the archaeological zone (10–5, Adm). Leaving the site you can go east on 117 to where it meets highway 119 which will take you back south to Puebla and highway 190 (or 150/150D to Veracruz).

Tizatlán (tee-saht-lahn') means "place of white earth." The site was studed by A. Caso between 1927 and 1935. In 1348 the city of Tlaxcala was established by a *Chichimec* group which became known as Tlaxcalans, and whose ruler was Xicoténcatl. The city eventually developed into a major trade center and was itself a wool-weaving town. Today, part of the ruins of the palace, built on a small platform, can be seen. Most interesting, however, are the small sanctuaries with two rectangular altars with murals painted on the sides. The original colors (red, yellow, ochre, blue and black) can still be seen, and the style is strongly similar to that of the Mixteca-Puebla. These paintings represent the story of the Tlaxcalan wars against the *Aztecs* who never succeeded in conquering them or incorporating them into their empire. There are also pictures of eagles, jaguars, scorpions and fish, and of the gods Tezcatlipoca and Tlaloc. Much of the stone used in the church in town is from the original structures of Tizatlán. Several areas are partially excavated, revealing portions of stuccoed buildings.

You can retrace your route to Puebla where you can double back west on 190 to **Cholula**. If you did not turn off at San Martín, 30k/18.5m farther on there is an exit to **Cholula**. Buses leave from Mexico City's east terminal every 15 minutes for Puebla. From here buses leave from 4 poniente at 3 norte. The Tourist Office in Puebla (5 Oriente, 3) will also arrange a trip for you.

  Cholula (cho-loo'-lah: 9–5; Adm.) has offered perhaps the greatest archaeological challenge of the various known sites. E. Noguera made the first serious attempts in 1931, and others like I. Marquina continued his efforts. Excavations have been going on regularly since 1967. At first glance, Cholula looks like a small mountain with a church on top of it. It is, in fact, a series of pyramids built one over the other. As each new culture took over, or as the 52-year cycle ended, a new structure was built. The area was inhabited by 600 B.C. when Nahua groups came from Ticomán and **Cuicuilco** and continued to be an important center up to the time of the arrival of the Spaniards. The first pyramid, called Tepanapa and built in 400 A.D., was 17 meters high and was decorated with red, blue and yellow mythological creatures. **Teotihuacán** influence was strong here, and when that city was destroyed, migrants settled in Cholula (650 A.D.). There were also commercial and artistic ties with **El Tajín** and the *Mixtec* area to the south. A group known as the "historic Olmecs" took over Cholula around 800 A.D. They were a tri-ethnic group composed of *Nahua*, *Mixtec* and *Chocho-Popolaca* tribes. They began to develop their own architectural and pottery styles, in some ways a mestization of many individual ones. The rise of a true culture is generally attributed to Huemoc who ruled from 1098 to the middle of the twelfth century. When **Tula** was destroyed, many of the *Toltecs* settled in Cholula, and this brought new influences including the warrior-like attitude of the people and the use of skulls and skeletons as a decorative motif.

  One of the significant and valuable things produced by the Mixteca-Puebla culture is the series of codices which reveal a great deal about the people and Pre-Columbian culture in general. These "books" or series of drawings detail customs of various kinds, especially religious customs. They are an American counterpart to Egyptian hieroglyphics—pictures which reveal aspects of life and history when they are "interpreted." The codices (codex is the singular) Borgia, Fejéváry-Mayer, Vaticanus B and the Mexican Manuscript No. 20 of the National Library in Paris were all made by the Mixteca-Puebla people.

Like so many other groups, the inhabitants of the Cholula region fell under the domination of the *Aztecs* except for one group, the Tlaxcalans at **Tizapán**. One of Cortés' fiercest fights was at Cholula. Its rulers and noblemen were killed, not because of the Spanish victory, but because they continued secretly plotting the overthrow and destruction of the Spaniards and their plans were discovered. The Tlaxcalans, on the other hand, welcomed the Spaniards and became their staunch allies in the attacks on **Tenochtitlán**, even saving Cortés' life on the famous "Noche triste" (sad night) when he had to retreat from the Aztec capital. The Tlaxcalans were rewarded by not having to pay tribute to Spain during the colonial period.

By 1519 the region around Cholula had 100,000 inhabitants, and there were reportedly nearly 400 temples and shrines in the area. Each group had added altars, priests' quarters, plazas, etc. to the main center. The final conglomerations of all of these things resulted in a "pyramid" covering 160,000 square meters: 400 meters long and nearly 60 meters high. The visitor may go through part of the six kilometers of tunnels in the pyramid and see parts of the underlying structures. At the base of the pyramid excavations constantly bring to light temple platforms, plazas, houses, sculptures, tombs, etc. Across the road on the north side of the pyramid you will find a small museum (Tue–Sat, 10–5) and a few more ruins.

In Puebla itself the Anthropology Museum is in the Civic Center built between the two forts on the hill at the north end of town (Tue–Sun, 10–4:30). There is a splendid new Amparo Museum on 2 Sur with 9 Oriente (Weds–Mon, 10–6) which has all of the former Regional Museum collection. As a point of interest, 20k/12m southeast of Puebla around what today is a lake and dam called Valsequillo, some of the oldest evidences of human settlement in Mexico were found (5000 B.C.).

Highway 190 goes south from Puebla to Izúcar de Matamoros, and southeast from there. There are several archaeological sites along this Route (e.g. Yachatío and Yucuñudahui) but they are not yet open to the public.

About 30k/18m farther on you come to Nochixtlan. 5k/2.5m west of here is the town of San Juan Yucuita which has a museum in the city hall with artifacts from around this region. Shortly before you reach Oaxaca you will come to Etla (right). A dirt road southwest from here leads to San José Mogote (2k) where there is a museum of pottery, stone and shell objects. The site itself existed before **Monte Albán**, and *Olmec* ceramics have been found here. Some platforms and rooms remain.

A2—VIA PUEBLA-TEHUACÁN (565K/351M)

The first leg of this trip, as far as Puebla, is the same as that given above in A1. From Puebla take the free highway 150 to Tehuacán (127k/79m) which can also be reached by bus from Mexico City's east terminal. There is a museum located in an old convent next to the church of Carmen on Reforma street, exhibiting some of the early corn cobs and other artifacts, and excellent diagrams of the development of the 516 sites which have been identified in the Tehuacán valley. The zone of archaeological interest lies to the south. There are four pyramids in the region, one each at Ajalpan (21k/13m), Calipan (36k/22m) and **Coxcatlán** (40k/25m) along highway 131 to Telixtlahuaca, and the fourth (named Cuta) about five minutes down a gravel road at the entrance to the town of Zapotitlán (27k/17m), on highway 125 south to Huajuapan. The desert around Zapotitlán is filled with all kinds of marine fossils since this was once the sea bed. Both highways join 190 to Oaxaca.

Coxcatlán (cosh-kaht-lahn') became famous through the excavations of R. MacNeish, who made 35 of them there, producing 10,000 artifacts in the process, to say nothing of the 26,000 corn cobs found. One, 5,600 years old, proved to be the ancestor of maize, thereby answering a question which had haunted archaeologists and historians of Pre-Hispanic America for a long time: the origin of corn, or maize. Also found were cave burials from 6000 B.C. which revealed ritual burials (offerings in baskets), cremation and cannibalism. Knotted nets also reveal the growth and use of cotton as early as 2000 B.C., and perhaps before that. Two large idols found in the vicinity in 1902 by E. Seler indicate that higher cultures inhabited the area later on.

A3—VIA CUAUTLA (510K/318M)

The first part of this route is slightly different from that of 6-A1 and offers some spectacular scenery between Ayotla and Cuautla, and two different archaeological sites. Take the free highway 190 to where it meets highway 115. Turn south (right). 7k/4m farther on you come to Chalco. In the Casa de la Cultura on Av. Cuauhtémoc 2. *Mexica* and other pieces are on display. Toward the end of highway 115 you will pass by Ozumba, a village dating from Pre-Hispanic times, which has a pyramid 30 meters high of *Aztec* construction. If it is a clear day you will get some splendid views of two of Mexico's most famous volcanoes: Iztaccihuatl (The Sleeping Woman, 17,338ft) and Popocatépetl (17,876ft). Drive through Cuautla to highway 160. 21k/12m east of Cuautla, a paved road to the right will take you 2 kilometers to Tepalcingo. Go left 3k to Chalcatzingo to the main plaza. Continue on an unpaved road for 300 meters and turn right. It is 2k to the archaeological area of **Chalcatzingo** (chal-caht-sing'-go: Tue–Sun, 10–5).

The name means "place of little circles" and was discovered by E. Guzmán in 1934. R. Piña Chan studied the site in 1955, and D. Grove in 1972. J. Angulo did some of the excavation and restoration work. This very old settlement at the base of two imposing hills dates from 1300 B.C. It was probably a religious center, but may also have been a control point for trade and commerce. It was influenced by different cultures until around 1200 A.D. The site is divided into four sections. Section IV is visited first, and has a circular stone altar and stelae at a partly uncovered pyramid platform base. An uphill walk of some fifty meters to section I-B brings you to the *Tlahuica* sanctuary built below the *Olmec* type relief sculptures called "The Warriors." Other carvings portray agriculture, rain, fertility (using the jaguar) and militarism, and are the only Olmec carvings to be found in this region of the central highlands. Others are still farther up the hill at sections I-A and II. Back down at section III there are the remains of two pyramids, a partially excavated ball court, an Olmec altar and late pre-classic stela. It takes at least an hour to visit the whole site without stopping too long at any one place.

Back at the paved road where you turned toward the ruins, you can turn left and go one kilometer to the **Las Pilas** recreation center where partially excavated very early structures can be seen (Tue–Sun, 9–5). The town is known as Jonacatepec.

These ruins came to light when a swimming pool and recreation site was created here. Excavations were begun in 1975 under the direction of J. Angulo. Several sets of stairs, some retaining walls and the bases of some platform structures have been uncovered. The construction is remarkably similar to the "talud" form of **Monte Albán**. This center was undoubtedly inhabited by the same group as nearby **Chalcatzingo**, and possibly from the same early dates (300–700 A.D.).

Once you are back on highway 160 again, it is 41k/26m to Izúcar de Matamoros where you join Route 6-A1 and highway 190.

A4—VIA CUERNAVACA-CUAUTLA (527K/329M)

This route begins by taking highway 95 or 95D south from Mexico City to Cuernavaca. If you want to go on into the city, it is possible to visit both the museum and the site of **Teopanzolco**, near the railroad station. A stopover in Cuernavaca would also enable you to visit **Xochicalco**. Both of these sites are described in Route 7. From Cuernavaca you take highway 160 to Cuautla. If Cuernavaca is not in your plans, then just before you reach the city limits there is a road (left) to Tepoztlán (14k/9m), the town made famous by Robert Redfield's anthropological studies there, and Carleton Beal's *Mexican Maze*. On the hill overlooking this city are the ruins of **Tepozteco** (tay-post-tay-'ko). It is a long, somewhat difficult climb to the top. At a steady, slow pace it takes about an hour. Many tourists of all ages do it, but you need good legs and a fairly strong heart (Tue–Sun, 9–5; Adm.).

Francisco Rodríguez called attention to the site in 1895, and E. Seler published an article on it in 1898. The pyramid temple was built around 1250 A.D. by the Tlahuicas whose capital was Cuanahuac (Cuernavaca) and who also built **Teopanzolco**. The temple honors the god of pulque, Ometotochtli (Two Rabbits) or Tepoztecatl, a name closer to the actual name of the site. The *Aztecs* under Ahuitzotl undertook to rebuild the sanctuary and they finished just before the emperor died in 1502. The structure is 10 meters high and there are still about 2½ meters of the temple walls left. A bench along the sanctuary wall is covered with cosmic signs, and there are also images related to war and sacrifice. If the temple site is not extraordinary, the view from the 600 meter hill is. At the bottom of the ridge there is a ball court, and there is a museum on the street behind the parish church in what was a 16th-century convent (Tue–Sun, 10–2, 4–6).

Leaving Tezpoztlán take the same road you came on and continue east. About 3 kilometers farther on it will join a highway going southeast to Cuautla. The rest of the route is identical with 6-A3 above.

There is a site between 6-A2 and 6-A3/4 for backpackers and rugged outdoor types—a very well preserved and imposing fortress site built into a hill surrounded by steep cliffs. It is located in the mountains 12k/7m from Tepexi de Rodríguez which is 46k/29m south of highway 150 (the turnoff is just before Cuapiaxtla), or 59k/37m north of Petalcingo on highway 190. There is a rough dirt and gravel road from Tepexi to the base of the hill. The approach on foot is from the south side. Several people in the village are willing to serve as guides.

Although the site was known already in 1807 through Dupaix, the first archaeological work was not done until 1965-66 by Gorenstein. During the 1970's E. Merlo began cleaning and preserving the ruins. A Dumaine did a little work in 1981-82, and in 1988-89 enough funds were received to complete the restoration work.

The site was occupied from 1300 to 1537 first by a *Toltec* group and then by the Popolacas who conquered **Cholula**, and finally by the *Mixtecs*. The settlement is on five different levels, supported by walls ranging from 5 to 20 meters in height of perfectly fitted and worked stone blocks. In places it can be seen that these were once stuccoed over and painted red, blue and yellow. The house rooms have walls 3 meters high and are well preserved. Outside the fortress, tombs have been found very similar to the *Mixtec* construction of stone walls with niches. Polychrome pottery was found in some of them. In one tomb painted with cinnabar (labeled no. 3) a high-ranking personage was buried, and nine skulls were found, possibly of persons who were funeral sacrifices. The setting and the state of preservation make this a truly fascinating site.

6-B: OAXACA AND NEARBY SITES

Oaxaca and the surrounding region offers much of archaeological interest and importance. In the city itself there is the Regional Museum. It is located in the former Dominican convent next to Santo Domingo church on Alcalá. It contains many of the treasures found in the sites nearby. The gold room is dazzling, especially the jewelry found in tomb 7 at **Monte Albán** (Tue–Sun, 10–5; Adm.).

On Calle Morelos 503, two blocks north of the main plaza, there is another fine museum, the Tamayo Museum of Pre-Hispanic Art. Its five galleries offer an array of some 800 pieces of the *Mixtec*, *Zapotec* and *Totonac* cultures (Weds–Mon, 10–2, 4–7; Sun 10–3; Adm.).

At this point, it would be good to say something about the first two cultures, since these were the people who inhabited the many sites in the Oaxaca region. In chronological order, the *Zapotecs* come first.

Tzapoteca is the nahuatl word for the zapote tree which these people claimed was the origin of their ancestors. According to one historian, the name they had for themselves was Ben-Zoa, or "cloud people". Both the tree legend and the cloud reference are found in the *Mixtec* culture and the later fusion of these two groups may have brought about the similarity as to their origins.

As early as 3,000 B.C. people were living in the Oaxaca valley region. Between 600 and 200 B.C. although there was no social unity as yet, there evidently were settled communities and they produced coarse, heavy ceramics. Between 200 B.C. and 200 A.D. a Zapotec style began forming, influenced by cultures to the south which brought such things as tripod vases. The most important settlement was **Monte Albán** which became a major ceremonial center during this time and probably something of an urban center as well.

Teotihuacán and *Maya* influences found their way into this region and were incorporated into the growing civilization. From 350 to 600

Monte Albán went through what is now designated as phase IIIA, experiencing the multiplication of structures and above all a very elaborate cult of the dead, shown by the exceptionally fine tombs made for them, and the sumptuous offering left with their bodies. The Zapotecs, meanwhile, spread southward and took Tehuantepec and other centers in that area. The people there today still speak the Zapotec language.

Between 700 and 1000 (phase IIIB) the **Zaachila** dynasty came into power and made Teozapotlán their capital. It became a theocratic state, and the high priest was often the real authority. Pitao (The Great One) was honored as the supreme god; the rain god was worshipped under four different forms. Human sacrifice was apparently rare, but the Zapotecs have the dubious honor of originating the Xipe-Totec ceremony of the flaying of a sacrificial victim and the high priest wearing the human skin for ceremonial purposes. During this period there were contacts with the *Maya* cities and perhaps this is how the bar-and-dot system of counting spread to the Maya world. The Zapotecs had their own calendar which was made of 260 days in four divisions of 65, these in turn being divided into five groups of thirteen. In 650 A.D. Zapotec astronomers had gone to **Xochicalco** for the unique meeting at which representatives of various cultures synchronized their calendars. Zapotec writing in picture form on deerskins also became a fine art. In addition to **Zaachila**, the Zapotecs built the city of Mictlán (**Mitla**) with its magnificent architectural sculpture.

Enter the *Mixtecs*. The Nahua name for this group is Mishtékall which means "cloud people," those who lived in Mixtlán, or "cloud land," that is, the high mountain regions. These people called themselves the Nusabi or "people of the rain." They originally inhabited the area covered today by northwestern Oaxaca, eastern Guerrero and southern Puebla. Legend says that their ancestors were born from trees in the present village of Achiutla. There were certainly people living in caves in the general area around 3,000 B.C. By 600 B.C. they had banded together and established the center of Monte Negro (modern name) which had such sophisticated things as planned streets and public construction. From 200 B.C. to 200 A.D. they spread to other centers like Tiltepec and Huamelulapan. In the next four centuries places like Yatachío and **Yucuñudahui** came under their influence. In the eighth century the important cities of Tilantongo and Coixlahuaca were founded. In the former was born one of the greatest Mixtec rulers, Eight Deer Tiger Claw (1011–1063) who brought all of the Mixtec centers under his rule and established an "empire," and who died (willingly) as a sacrificial victim.

In the earlier history the Mixtecs had been influenced by **El Tajín**, especially in their art and architecture which made much use of the

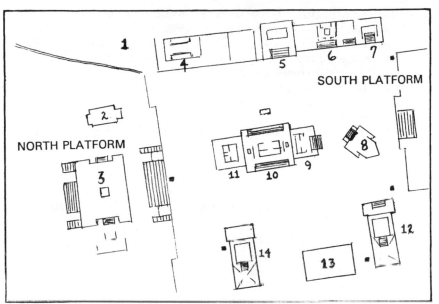

MONTE ALBAN

1. parking area
2. building A
3. sunken patio
4. ball court
5. mound P
6. palace
7. mound O

8. mound J - observatory
9. mound I
10. building H - central pyramid
11. mound/building G
12. mound M
13. "Dancers" temple
14. System IV
    stela

"greca" or squared-off spiral, so prominent in the fret work at **Mitla**. They were fine potters and excellent goldsmiths and craftsmen in semiprecious stones. Their flint-edged swords, padded armor and reed shields enhanced their military prowess and the Aztecs never did completely subdue them nor take all of their territory. But the Mixtecs themselves were pushed southward by the *Toltecs* and *Chichimecs*. They eventually got to the Oaxaca region where they clashed with the Zapotecs who abandoned Monte Albán and moved to centers farther south such as **Yagul**, and **Lambityeco**. The Mixtecs intermingled with the peoples they conquered, particularly the Zapotecs. A semi-alliance was brought about between the two groups when a Zapotec king married a Mixtec lady in 1280. Much of their history has been preserved in their codices, paintings made on deerskins in somewhat the same way as the Egyptians made hieroglyphics. There are four of these, known as the Bodley, Nuttall, Selden and Vienna Codices. They reveal various customs and culture traits such as the calendar cycle of feasts, ritual sacrifice, the cult of the dead and a royal geneology starting in 692 A.D.

Not even the combined Mixtec and Zapotec forces could hold back the Aztecs who invaded under Axayácatl in the middle of the fifteenth century. They did succeed in turning back Ahuitzotl at **Guiengola**, and the last Zaachila king, Cocijo-eza, married Ahuitzotl's daughter, thereby bringing about a lasting alliance and peace. The son of this marriage, Cocijo-pij, was the last Zapotec ruler. He died in 1563 long after the Spaniards had taken over the Oaxaca region. Mixtec rule also came to an end with the Spanish conquest. Cortés, in fact, was given the title "Marquis of Oaxaca" and forty thousand square kilometers of the region as his personal property!

Now that we have seen something of the cultures, here's how you get to the two "capitals" mentioned.

6B-1 Take Flores Magón street (or 20 de Noviembre) south from the main plaza to the Outer Loop. Turn right here and you will see a sign directing you across a little bridge. Once you cross it, the paved road to the right goes 8k/5m to **Monte Albán**. Buses leave for the site from Hotel Mesón del Angel on Calle Mina between Díaz Ordaz and Mier y Terán streets 6 times a day.

Monte Albán (moan'tay ahl-bahn': 8–5, Adm. except Sun) means "green hill." It was one of the most important centers south of Mexico City. A. Caso (there is a monument to him at the entrance) worked here in 1931–32 (the year the famous Tomb 7 was found), and again in 1935 with J. Acosta. Many other archaeologists have visited and investigated the site. Neither they nor all historians agree on the evolution of Monte Albán, but it is generally accepted that it took place in four major stages, the third divided into two periods. In the museum on the grounds there are explanations of the historical and cultural development of the area. The first is from 1000 to 300 B.C. *Olmec* people were here around 700 B.C. as the figures on the Temple of the Dancers (erroneously named) indicate. These figures represent ball players (one plausible interpretation) and have the characteristic semi-negroid Olmec features and the "helmet" head-coverings. Another interpretation has it that these are prisoners who have been slain. The bar-and-dot system found at **Tres Zapotes** on the gulf coast is also seen here.

The temple (see map, no. 13) and the substructures of the north platform (3) were built at this time. Between 300 and 100 B.C. the huge area which had been levelled off on top of the hill (940 x 440 meters) was laid out and the plaza was paved. The pentagonal edifice J (8) was built, probably for astronomical purposes, and stones from the Dancers' temple were reused in other constructions. The period from 100 B.C. to 950 A.D. saw the rise of Zapotec culture. The north temple was rebuilt, ball courts (4) were added, and structures were built using stone slabs as terrace walls and having wide cornices at the top. The central platforms (9, 10, 11) were added for the temples to the gods of rain, fire and the bat god. Mound three on the south platform was excavated in 1989 and revealed that it was constructed around the middle of the 8th century A.D. Elaborate tombs were constructed, and over 150 of them have been found. The quantity of valuable articles buried with the dead shows a strong cult of the dead. Tomb 7 had over 500 articles in it. During this period there was commerce with **Teotihuacán** and with the Maya region and it is reflected in the art forms and in borrowed gods. As might be suspected, pottery forms range from simple monochrome ware to elaborate effigy forms. The ceramic figures of rulers and priests in their highly ornamental headdresses and jewelry strongly resemble similar figures found in coastal cultures of Colombia and Ecuador. Around 800 A.D. the Mixtecs began moving into Zapotec territory and they eventually took over Monte Albán. They brought with them Toltec influences, including its militarism, and an age of decline set in. The Zapotecs and Mixtecs intermarried but there was no strong cultural revival, and both groups were overrun by the Aztecs and incorporated into their empire.

6B-2 Using the same exit from Oaxaca as described in 6-B1, when you cross the bridge take the left road. It is about 14k/9m to **Zaachila**. Buses to the site leave from Miguel Carrera and Arista Streets in Oaxaca.

Zaachila (sah-chee'-lah: 10:30–5:30; Adm) was originally called Tzapotecapan, or "seat of government." The Aztecs called it Teozapotlan. The Mixtecs of Cuilapan came from Yanhuitlán to Zaachila and in 1280 the Zapotec king married a Mixtec lady bringing about a semi-alliance of the two groups. Later Cocijo-eza (1482–1529) did the same kind of thing by marrying an Aztec princess. This whole geneology is found on the "Lienzo de Guevea," a sixteenth-century manuscript.

There are a number of mounds in this former capital, but today the visitor can see only the massive earth mound which has two tombs on top. One of them may be that of Eight Deer Fire Serpent, born around 1400. There were nine bodies in the antechamber, persons sacrificed at the time of the burial. This site was excavated in 1962 and 1965 by R. Gallegos, but with the protection of soldiers, since the local inhabitants are against any archaeological work being carried on, basically out of fear of disturbing the dead and arousing wrathful spirits. In one mound there were twenty-five burials, one of which was a person who had been sacrificed. Clay urns of the Monte Albán II type and other kinds of pottery have been found, as well as various types of jewelry. Most of what has been found in the area is in the museum in Oaxaca.

Many of the sites which will be mentioned in Route 6-C can also be visited in a day's trip from Oaxaca, and even several on the same day.

6-C: OAXACA TO CIUDAD CUAUHTÉMOC AND THE GUATEMALA BORDER (785K/491M)

The only bus line which covers this whole route is "Cristóbal Colón." It can also be taken from Mexico City's south or east stations. Only 24k/15m from Oaxaca you will see the familiar sign indicating an archaeological zone to the right. Buses from Oaxaca to Mitla or Tlacolula will stop here. There is a dirt-rock road for 1k to **Dainzú** where archaeological work is still going on and has brought to light a fascinating ceremonial center at the base of a rugged hill (10–5; Adm).

Dainzú (dine-soo'), discovered relatively recently, was excavated by I. Bernal in 1966. It dates from around 600 B.C. and may be one of the final traces of the *Olmecs* in the Oaxaca region. There are indications that the site was occupied until at least 900 A.D. The huge pyramid structure (54 x 42 meters) set against the hill is impressive, but the most interesting feature is the ball court and the art work portraying ball players—very similar to the famous "danzantes" of **Monte Albán**. This would show that the ball game dates to early pre-classic times and perhaps had a different form. The humanized jaguars also fit in with the *Olmec* culture. There are some fifty carved stones at the base of the pyramid (several of them have been cemented into the base as part of the restoration process). They were made around 300 B.C. As the excavations progress they reveal large complexes of structures. This may have been a regular city and not only a ceremonial center.

5k/3m farther on, you will see **Lambityeco** right on the highway to your right. Test pits and trenches are still being worked on. The buses to Mitla and Tlacolula will stop here (9–5; Adm).

This is also a relatively recent discovery. J. Paddock worked here in 1968 and excavations are still going on. There are over two hundred mounds in the area. To date, excavations have brought to light two temples, two platform structures and multi-chambered houses. One was found which had a tomb under it, with a sculpture and name-glyph of the occupant. Several houses also had "pictures" of their owners in sculpted stucco. The structures seem to date from the time that **Monte Albán** was abandoned by the *Zapotecs*, but the site itself existed much earlier. Some *Maya* influence has been noted in the sculpture techniques, particularly the use of "grecas" (the Greek spiral which is squared off) which are also found at **Mitla** and other places in the Oaxaca region.

A little farther on you will pass the town of Tlacolula. Another 7k/3.5m will bring you to a paved road (left) which goes to **Yagul**, a small city protected by hilltop fortifications (8–6; Adm).

Yagul (yah-ghoul': 8–6, Adm.) in Zapotec language means "old town." A. F. Bandelier described this site in 1881. The Colegio de México excavated here in 1946–47; I. Bernal in 1954 and 1965; and J. Paddock in 1965. This site at first appeared to be basically a civic rather than religious center, but excavations have revealed many indications of a ritual and ceremonial nature also. People lived in the valley as early as 3000 B.C. Around 400 B.C. there was influence from **Monte Albán**, and a number of tombs from this period have been found (e.g., Tomb 32). The overall construction is like a labyrinth of rooms, or a huge palace with six patios.

Part of the red stucco floor is still visible in places. Tombs were found in the Patio de la Rana (Frog Patio). In some cases there are two or three tombs together (as in Patio 4) with a common antechamber. They were covered with rectangular slabs with small holes through which ropes were passed to lower them into place. Stone mosaic work found here is similar to that of **Mitla**, but interior. It was used especially for the decoration of tombs. About 900 A.D. there was a building boom for a time, fostered by the **Zaachila** dynasty. When the *Mixtecs* began to move into the valley, a fortress was constructed on the hill overlooking the site. It was abandoned around 1519 A.D. The ball court here is larger than the one at **Monte Albán** and is in excellent condition. In spite of its basically "urban" character, the repeated use of the skull motif, the elaborate tombs indicating a cult of the dead, and a large room with a stone altar are evidence that religious beliefs were also a part of the daily life at Yagul.

After another relatively short distance (10k/6m) you will come to the road (again to the left) which goes to **Mitla**, one of the most famous sites in southern Mexico. Don't miss the ruins on the north side of the church. There is also a small museum in the town plaza which you can pass on your way to the ruins (9–6). Mitla can also be reached by bus. They leave Oaxaca about every thirty minutes from Las Casas and Mier y Terán streets.

Mitla (meet'-lah: 8:30–6:30, Adm.) means "place of the dead," and is a corruption of Mictlan. W. Holmes described this site in 1895, and A. Caso and D. Rubin worked here in 1934–35. More recent work was done by I. Bernal (1961). Stone tools and other artifacts found in the area indicate that early settlers lived in the caves of this region between 5000 and 3000 B.C. It was a simple farming settlement for many centuries, and the site in question may have been originally a ceremonial center and a place where the dead were buried. Subterranean chambers contain cruciform tombs, but these were probably meant for the bodies of priests or rulers.

The cultural surge of Mitla came when the *Zapotecs* pressured by the *Mixtecs* found refuge here after fleeing from **Monte Albán**. The Mixtecs, however, eventually also took over Mitla. There are five main groups of buildings containing eleven rectangular courts, nine of them with buildings on all sides. The architectonic sculpture is one of the most striking features, and the "fret work" contains fourteen different motifs. The lintels across the door openings are monolithic, and weigh up to thirty tons. One such lintel is 6 meters long. The Hall of the Columns is 38 × 17 meters. In the patio of the tombs, the visible 2.80 meters column under one of the structures is known as the Pillar of Death, and legend says that if you hold your arms around it and can feel it move, death is imminent. The people of Mitla produced tripod polychrome pottery (with handles), all kinds of jewelry, rock crystal and alabaster vases and objects, mosaics, etc. Fine examples exist in the museum in Oaxaca and in the Frissel museum on the village plaza. Mitla was destroyed in 1494 by the *Aztec* king Ahuitzotl.

The next thing of significance is near Tehuantepec, if you are adventuresome. **Guiengola** was a *Zapotec* hilltop fortress where the early Tehuantepec inhabitants held out successfully against the *Aztecs* and other invaders until the Spaniards finally overwhelmed them. To get to this site you must take a gravel and dirt road from highway 190 (left) just outside the east end of the city. About 16k/10m farther on you will be at the base of a hill. You have to climb to the top; it will take about an hour, and you have to be in good physical condition.

Guiengola (variously misspelled Quiengola, Guengola, Giengola: ghee-yen-go'-lah) means "great rock." E. Seler described the site in 1896. Little archaeological work has been done here, though this was an important *Zapotec* hilltop stronghold from 1000 to 1300 A.D. which the Aztecs were never able to conquer. Buildings are scattered over the hilltop where small terraces were used (or made) for constructions. There is a central place 150 meters long surrounded by several pyramid bases. One of these may have been the palace of the Zapotec king Cocijo-eza. One structure has a vertical face platform superimposed by three sloping tiers. There is no question that while this was a fortress it was also a religious center. Near one plaza there is a ball court. Most of the architecture is of stone slabs set with mortar and covered with a stucco finish, apparently once painted red. Some of this still remains. This center probably began around 300 A.D. and it lasted until the Spanish forces subdued it in the 1520's.

26k/15m from Tehuantepec you come to the town of Juchitán. A museum on Colón and Juárez streets has 300 *Zapotec* and *Mixtec* artifacts. A little farther north you meet the junction with highway 185 going north. This is a good, fast 181k/113m highway across the isthmus for those who want to head toward Veracruz and the gulf coast or Yucatán areas to join Routes 1 and 2. 90k/56m farther on at Tapanatepec you will come to highway 200. We will come back to this road to the border afterwards. A short distance from here on highway 190, you enter the state of Chiapas.

This large, southeastern state of Mexico is generally divided into four areas: the Pacific coast, the Sierra Madre mountains, the central plateau and the central depression. The eastern part of the state is covered with tropical rain forest and portions of it are almost impenetrable. In this area are the *Maya* centers of **Bonampak**, **Palenque**, Piedras Negras and **Yaxchilán**. The mountain area is interesting for the many tribes in the Tuxtla Gutiérrez and San Cristóbal de las Casas regions. These cities are at the head of the central depression. There are numerous sites in the mountains but most are inaccessible as are those in the areas of dense rainfall.

A publication of the National Institute of Anthropology and History lists 1498 archaeological sites in the state. Some of these are pre-ceramic and pre-classic and go back to at least 7000 B.C. (e.g. Santa Marta cave).

The next major town is Tuxtla Gutiérrez. The Regional Museum is on 885 Calzada de los Hombres Ilustres which runs west from Parque Madero at 11 Ote and 5 Nte (Tues.–Sat., 9–4; Adm.). Much of the pottery and sculpture from the local area and different from that seen elsewhere is housed here. The Hotel Bonampak has copies of the famous murals at that site (see Route 2-B2). This town is also a gathering place for the Indians from nearby villages, and you will see all different kinds of native costumes being worn and hear different dialects being spoken. This is an ethnologist's paradise and an anthropological treat.

East of Tuxtla Gutiérrez about 32k/20m you will come to some reconstructed ruins right on the highway and the road which leads to the town and ruins of **Chiapa del Corzo**. Follow the paved road through town to where it meets a dirt road. It is a short distance to the archaeological site.

The town of **Chiapa del Corzo** (chee-ah'-pah day core'-so) was founded by Diego de Mazariegos in 1528 on the site of an old Indian capital called Nendiume. This center was an important exchange point for Pre-Columbian trade between **Teotihuacán** and the Petén (Guatemala) areas farther south. A Tulane University archaeological team excavated at the site in 1940 and the New World Archaeological Foundation did extensive work in 1961. All of this work has resulted in a rather remarkable chronology. This may have been a settlement as early as 4500 B.C., but six rather clear phases of development began in 1500 B.C. The third phase, from 450 to 200 B.C. shows influences of **Monte Albán**. In the following period, to 600 A.D., the Chiapanecs arrived and pushed back the *Mayas* during their expansion period. At the site there are detailed plans and descriptions on display. Five periods in the development of pottery have also been identified, with fifteen distinctive types. The Ocos style, about 1450 B.C. seems to resemble that of Ecuador and may indicate some Pacific coastal contacts. Most of the structures are of mud faced with river stones, in some cases covered over with a limestone surface in stucco fashion. The small structures on the highway are somewhat different from the low stepped platforms and two-tiered structures at the site itself.

The next important town, San Cristóbal de las Casas, like Tuxtla Gutiérrez is the gathering place of different Indian groups, and from that point of view is fascinating. For the archaeology "bug" however, the important place is a hacienda northeast of town on Guerrero street called "Na Balom" (The Sign of the Jaguar). This was the home of Franz Blom, one of the early outstanding *Maya* scholars, and one of the first who recognized the importance of the Chiapas region. He spent years working here and turned his home into a museum which is unique in many ways since it also houses a large library of works related to the ethnology and archaeology of the region. For the Pre-Columbianist a visit to the Blom museum is a real treat (Tues.–Sun. 4–5:30 p.m.).

In the stretch between San Cristóbal and the border there are many ruins, most of them of *Maya* origin. Few have been restored, however, and fewer still made accessible to the ordinary traveler. There are some possibilities, however.

A few miles past Teopisca, 32k/20m from San Cristóbal, there is a road to Las Rosas. Near here is Cerro Chavín where there are fort-like ruins.

Cerro Chavín (say'-rrow chah-veen') is a small, late classic (900 A.D.) Maya site studied by R. M. Adams in 1960. Built on a high hill,

surrounded by cliffs, this fortress is a fine example of military instal-
lations at the end of the classic period, and perhaps a key to the
answer of why the Maya cities and civilization disappeared.

Farther south on highway 190, in the hills to the left, is a reported site
known as **Yerba Buena**. At the north end of Comitán, the **Hun Chabin**
(hoon chah-bean') ruins are located.

The site was investigated in 1940 by the Tulane University archaeological team. It had previously been studied by Franz Blom in 1926–
27. This is a late classic *Maya* site and consists of several tiered
structures around a plaza. A number of secondary burials have been
found in nearby caves. Artifacts from the site are in the Blom museum
at San Cristóbal de las Casas.

24k/15m south of the city a paved road (left) goes to Lagunas de
Montebello. Close to the lake is a classic age settlement, **Chinkultic**.

Chinkultic means "little sanctuary." E. Solor visited this site in
1901, and S. Morley in 1938. Tulane University worked here in 1940
and T. Proskouriakoff in 1950. This site existed into the late classic
period. It may have been a trade route spot on the important north-
south lines of communication between 600 and 1200 A.D. There are
four groups of ruins, and evidences of plazas surrounded by mounds,
few of which have been excavated. The main pyramid of four tiers has
a stairway 60 meters high. A burial was found at the level of the 20th
step, and three burial vaults were in front of the pyramid. There is a
"cenote" at the site, called Agua Azul, used for offerings. The ball
court had an elegant marker and the sculptured monuments found
here are of superior quality. One beautiful stone disc is in the museum in Mexico City, and some ten stelae were discovered.

From the turnoff to this last site it is 70k/44m to Ciudad Cuauhtémoc
and the border.

VIA HIGHWAY 200 TO TAPACHULA-TALISMÁN (from Oaxaca 675k/424m)

130k/81m east of Tehuantepec highway 200 runs southeast to the
border. From this highway junction it is 288k/180m. The whole region
between the highway and the ocean is virtually unexplored archaeologically, though at least thirty-eight sites have been discovered and
studied. Most are shell middens; a few sites give evidence of some
simple structured remains. Many of the towns along this route are very
old, and pottery has been found which some believe shows traces of
Olmec influence, while others see more of the *Toltec-Maya* characteristics. These towns include **Tonalá**, Huixtla, Huehuetán and Mazatán.

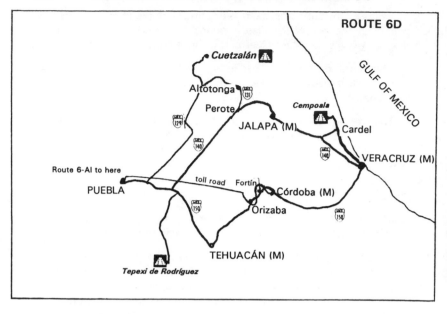

The **Tonalá** (toe-nah-lah') ruins are on a mountainside 13k/8m northwest of the town. P. Drucker worked here in 1947, and E. N. Ferdon mapped the area in 1953. This religious center has several platforms 1 to 3½ meters high with unbalustraded central stairways, and in some cases stone paved ramps. One- to three-room structures on top served as temples. Two stone altars have been found, one with a jaguar head, the other with an alligator head. *Olmec*-style stelae have also been discovered, one with a bar-and-dot numeral on it. All of the architectural features indicate that this center was thriving before the Christian era began.

In Tonalá itself on Av. Hidalgo 177 there is a Regional Museum with some 3,000 pieces. Well worthwhile, especially if you don't want to climb to the ruins.

About 15k after you pass Huixtla, a road (right) goes to Mazatán. Prehistory investigations made in 1984–85 led in 1990 to archaeological exploration and study in the region around here, particularly at San Carlos and Paso de la Amada where mounds are revealing houses and artifacts dating from 1650–1500 B.C. There is nothing here to visit as yet, but this corroborates what was said at the beginning of this section.

About halfway between Tapachula and the border, a sign indicates the archaeological zone of **Izapa**, just off the highway to the left.

Izapa (ee-sah'-pah) is of great importance because it seems to provide a link between the *Olmec* and *Maya* civilizations. A number of archaeologists have studied the site, including M. Stirling in 1941, 1943 and 1945, P. Drucker in 1948, M. Coe in 1957 and R. Piña Chan in 1960. This may have been the ceremonial center for the people of nearby Tapachula, which dates from 1700 B.C. Eighty temple pyramids have been identified in the groups of mounds in the area. A ball court has also been discovered. *Olmec* influences are seen in some of the figures on the stelae, particularly those with the jaguar mask on top, or with a head inside the jaws of a jaguar. On the other hand, altars decorated with "cluttered scenes" in baroque fashion are more *Maya* in style. Some of the highland Maya groups from Guatemala certainly came through this area at various times. The visitor today can see several of the low platform structures in dark brown stone, and a few of the stelae. The site continues under excavation when funds permit.

In Tapachula the Socomusco Museum (a domed tin roof building sitting in a park) has some **Izapa** stelae and artifacts from Pacific coastal sites.

6-D: PUEBLA TO VERACRUZ (296K/185M; 344K/215M)

There are three highways to Veracruz from Puebla. The best and fastest, highway 150D (the toll road) has nothing of archaeological interest.

The second possible route is the regular highway 150, the free road, from which it is possible to visit the sites mentioned in routes 6-A1 and 6-A2. Farther on, there is a museum in the old colonial building on the corner of the plaza in Córdoba which also houses the Casa de la Cultura and the public library.

The third possible route has several things of archaeological interest and importance. Take highway 150 or 150D from Puebla 44k/27m to where highway 140 begins and runs northeast past Acatzingo to Perote. For the very adventuresome, there is an interesting side trip. Before reaching Perote you will come to Zacatepec where highway 129 begins. You can take this north 68k/42m to Zaragoza and from there a paved road goes 51k/32m to Cuetzalán where there is a small museum in the city hall, and another two-room museum on Calle 2 de Abril (10–2; 3–5) which houses the artifacts from the *Totonac* ruins of **Yohualichan** (yo-wah-lee'-chahn). Cuetzalán is also served by "Autotransportes Mexico-Texcoco" from Mexico City's east bus terminal. The ruins themselves are located 6k east by a dirt road and are on a promintory that overlooks the mountain highland.

These ruins, investigated by J. García Payón and D. Molina were the center of a Tajín culture from 200 to 650 A.D. The remains of the buildings show strong similarities to **El Tajín**, particularly the presence of niches in the various tiers of the pyramid structures. The *Totonac* presence is likewise seen in the yokes and pottery found here. The rough terrain was made level by the construction of large platforms on which the buildings stood. The limestone rock in the area made it possible to cut very large blocks. Some used in the ball court are more than 3 meters long. The court itself is one of the largest in Mesoamerica, nearly 90 meters long. The spectator stands are still evident, complete with stairways at each end. The site also contains housing units, at least two pyramids and several platforms. These were all covered with stucco and possibly painted. There is also stucco decoration in the form of the squared-off spiral. The *Toltecs* took over the center in the tenth century, and Nahua-speaking groups later displaced them. The people of the area today still speak Nahuatl and follow ancient customs, especially in dress. The *Aztecs* incorporated this site into the empire during the east-ward expansion.

Highway 140 continues from Perote to Jalapa which now has a splendid new museum. It is located on Av. Jalapa and 1o de Mayo. The collection, mainly of the *Olmec*, *Huastec* and *Totonac* cultures contains pottery, figurines, jewelry and small sculptures, especially Remojadas pieces (the so-called "smiling faces"), and several excellent larger sculptures.

Instead of following highway 140 directly into Veracruz, it is possible to turn left at Puente Nacional and go to Cardel and **Cempoala** as mentioned above in the second possible route.

For places of archaeological interest in the Veracruz area, see Route 1-B.

Route 7: Mexico City to Acapulco

The route south of Mexico City to the Pacific Ocean passes through two states: Morelos and Guerrero.

Morelos is Mexico's smallest state but it has several important archaeological sites. There were people living in this area by at least 1500 B.C. and possibly earlier. *Olmec*-related groups may have been among the first. **Chalcatzingo** seems to confirm this. Later *Toltecs* settled in the region. When the Nahua-speaking groups moved south and settled around Lake Texcoco, the *Tlahuicas* continued farther south and established Cuauhnáhuac, today Cuernavaca. The political power of the region was shared with the chief of Oaxtepec. The *Aztecs* incorporated both centers into their empire. When Cortés decided to attack **Tenochtitlán**, he undertook to subdue the *Tlahuicas* first to be sure he had no enemy at his back. The Tlahuicas came under Spanish control in April of 1521.

Guerrero is one of the least developed regions archaeologically. Part of the reason for this lies in the fact that this region of Mexico is rather thinly populated and settlements are few and far between. This makes finding any Pre-Columbian settlements even more difficult. Conversely, so much has come to light in other parts of Mexico that the rather limited funds for archaeology have been diverted to excavating and restoring those centers.

The state of Guerrero was created in 1847 and named after the famous independence hero Vicente Guerrero. It is hot, mountainous country which more than twenty different groups inhabited in Pre-Columbian times. Although there are many known sites, there has not been any thorough dig of a major site and very few scientific excavations have been made. When the Infernillo Dam was built on the Balsas river, the National Institute of Anthropology and History did some salvage archaeology (1966–67), confirming earlier reports of fairly advanced cultures in this region. The Spaniards came into the area mainly in search of the gold which these people had sent to the Aztecs as tribute and they established one major port as a contact with the Pacific world—Acapulco—where the Manila galleon dropped anchor once a year. It was originally called Navidad.

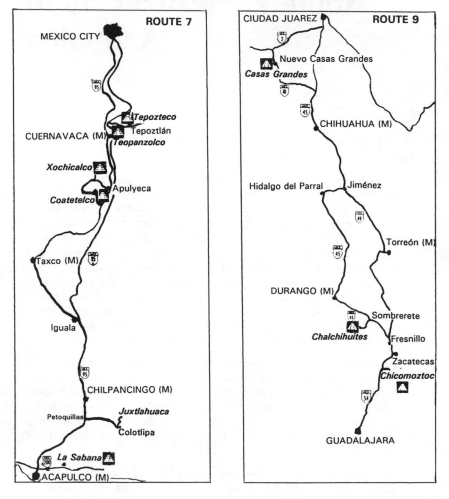

Cacahuamilpa and **Juxtlahuaca** caves indicate that people were living in Guerrero long before the Christian era. It is possible that the Tenocelome, or *Olmecs*, originated in this region. Finds from various sites indicate that there were contacts with several of the more advanced cultures—**Teotihuacán**, **Cholula** and the *Mixtecs* among them. These finds include some ball courts in the Balsas basin, isolated examples of stelae, clay figurines, earplugs, masks of jadite, Plumbate wares (originally from around the Mexico-Guatemala border) and *Toltec*-type pottery. Burials have been found in caves, simple graves, stone-lined tombs, urns and under houses. A very interesting type of effigy pottery has been found near Mezcala.

Some of the Guerrero sites, most of them not easily accessible, are: Acatepec, Arcelia, Balsas, Buenavista, Calera, Cañada, Cohayutla, Lagunillas, La Puerta, **La Sabana**, Mexcala, Ometepec, Oztocingo, Papanoa, Petatlán, Teloloapan (where there is a pyramid) and Zihuatanejo.

While some archaeological efforts have been made, most of the attention given to Guerrero has been by those trying to establish a relationship between this region and the highly developed cultures in other parts of Mexico. There is reason to believe, for instance, that the art of goldsmithing was imported through this area and first practiced here long before the Europeans arrived in Mexico. There has been some interest, also, in searching for contact points with Central and South America through ancient settlements along Guerrero's Pacific coast.

Highway 95 is the main artery for this route and has a free road and a toll road. The bus lines which covers all of these cities is Estrella de Oro (south terminal). Autos Pullman de Morelos and Líneas Unidas del Sur go as far as Cuernavaca and Cuautla. The free road detours west to Taxco (also spelled Tasco) and the total distance to Acapulco is 431k/268m. The toll road is 18k/13m shorter. These figures do not include any side trips to archaeological sites.

Shortly before you get to Cuernavaca, there is a road (left) which goes to Tepoztlán, 17k/11m. From the toll road it is possible to join highway 115D to Tepoztlán. On the hill overlooking this town are the ruins of **Tepozteco** (see Route 6 A4). Autos Pullman de Morelos leaves from Mexico City's south terminal several times a day.

In Cuernavaca itself there are two things. In the main square of the city is the Palacio de Cortés, built on top of a pyramid base and one of Mexico's oldest buildings which now houses the Cuauhnáhuac Museum. The archaeological exhibits are on the first floor. They come from various cultures, especially those of the region itself. (Tue–Fri, 11–6; Sat, Sun 11:30–1; Adm. except Sun.). From the museum, go a block left to the plaza and turn right onto Guerrero. Follow this all the way until it meets Farías; turn right and go to the next major intersection, cross it and continue on Cuaglia until it ends at Río Balsas. Turn right and follow it to where it seems to end. Turn right. You are still on Balsas. About six blocks farther on it will become Ronda. The entrance to the ruins of **Teopanzolco** are on this street.

Teopanzolco (tay-oh-pahn-soul'-ko: Tues.–Sun., 9–5; Adm.) was discovered during the Mexican Revolution when it was used as a site to mount cannons which shook the surface dirt loose revealing the structure below. It was excavated in 1922 by E. Noguera, and by R. Piña Chan in 1957. The Tlahuica Indians built this center around 1000 A.D. They had their capital in Cuahnáhuac (Cuernavaca). Later the *Aztecs* conquered the area and another pyramid was built on top of the first one. The site consists of a central plaza, the large pyramid structure, a smaller similar structure, several rectangular platforms and one circular platform. The latter were added by the conquerors from Tenochtitlán. Most of the building here took place between 1200 and 1500 A.D.

Take the free road 95 south to Alpuyeca (21k/13m). Here, highway 55 goes west 13k/8m to a paved road (right) which leads to **Xochicalco**, one of the finest sites south of Mexico City.

Xochicalco (show-chee-kahl'-ko: Tues–Sun., 9–5; Adm.) means "house of flowers," a delicate name for an impressive fortress town covering 620 acres. Around 300 A.D. people living in the area leveled off parts of a hill to make a large flat space for construction. They laid a plaza 350 × 200 meters and in the center built a platform structure with vertical walls 4 meters high. Some *Huastec* influence found its way here in the form of rock sculpture, a calendar and the cult of Quetzalcoatl.

In 650 A.D. *Maya* and *Zapotec* astronomers met here with local representatives to synchronize their calendars—a unique event in Pre-Hispanic history. Stelae were sculptured to commemorate the event, and on them figures hold representations of the dating system of the Mayas and Zaspotecs and of the *Mixtecs* and Nahuas. At this time Xochicalco experienced the influence of **Monte Albán**, and the central platform structure was rebuilt with the addition of the beautifully sculptured stone slabs as facing. The frieze on the left side of the stairway symbolizes the astronomical meeting mentioned above. The stone slabs are joined artistically by the eight undulating serpents. The human figures are Maya-type personages, and may indicate relationship with the later *Toltec* influences on the Yucatán peninsula. Around 800 A.D. the defense walls of the city were built against the "historic Olmecs" from Mixteca Baja. A structured society developed between 700 and 1000 A.D. with a priestly and noble class, weavers, stone masons, potters and other artisans, and merchants. Three other features should be noted: the ball court which is 51 meters long and 9 wide; the temple of the stelae, so named because three of them were found in a cavern under the floor, each 1.80 meters high; and the subterranean passages in the hill, some of them with paintings and one with a carved stone altar. Be sure you have a good flashlight with you if you intend to enter. E. Noguera worked at this site in 1947, and C. Sáenz between 1961 and 1967. Much of the reconstruction was done in 1961–62.

You can continue west and south on 55 to Mazatepec and **Coatetelco** (ko-ah-tay-tell'-ko).

This site was built by the *Tlahuicas* in 1400 A.D. There was originally a lake here, and many rock mounds. The name, in fact, means "the place of the snakes of the rock mounds." The present-day churches are built on the foundations of Pre-Hispanic buildings. Still to be seen are several temple platforms surrounding an I-shaped ball court. Some of the stucco floor is still visible. A museum here contains the artifacts found during the excavations done principally by R. Arana.

A short distance south of here you rejoin highway 95 to Taxco. At 1 Porfirio Delgado street you will find the Stratling Archaeological Museum (Tues.–Sat., 10–5; Adm.). The second and third floor of this museum have Pre-Columbian artifacts, mainly from the western part of Mexico.

Still farther south, Iguala and the capital city of this state, Chilpancingo are of much historical importance for Mexico's early independence years. In the former city hall of Chilpancingo *Olmec* artifacts are on display and pieces from the relatively new site of Colotlipa. 6k/4m south of the city you come to Petaquillas where there is a road (left) in rather poor condition, but passable except during the raining season. At the end of this road (55k/34m) is the little village of Colotlipa. In 1984 important ruins were found here which have been identified as the remains of an *Olmec* city. Excavations are going on and the area is closed off to visitors. From here another dirt road goes 4k into the mountains to the north to **Juxtlahuaca** (hoosh-lah-wah'-kah) cave. The entrance is 4 meters high and 5 meters wide. The cave is vast and should not be entered without a guide. Several people in Colotlipa are willing to perform this service. There are some 19 "rooms" along the known part of the cave. Depending on how much you want to see, a visit can take up to 4 or 5 hours.

This site came to the attention of the archaeological world after the visit of Carlo Gay and Gilbert Griffin in 1966. The cave had long been known but few knew about the paintings in it dating back 3000 years, making them some of the oldest in the New World. The drawings, located more than a kilometer into the cave, still show the black, green, red and yellow colors with which they were made. It has been suggested that the figures have a certain resemblance to the *Olmec* style, supporting the theory that this culture began in the Guerrero region of Mexico, rather than on the gulf coast where it later flourished. One drawing, on a stone slab, depicts a red serpent in combat with (?) a feline creature, early indication perhaps of two important religious cults. The recent finds of the "city" mentioned above strengthen the Olmec connection.

There are many similar caves in the region to the east as you continue to head toward the Pacific. In some of them the local people still offer annual sacrifices and hold religious ceremonies related particularly to agriculture. Just outside of Acapulco highway 200 crosses 95. There are several very old settlements to the west along this highway, where some archaeological probings have been made, especially Tecpan, Papnoa, Petetlán, Zihuatanejo and La Unión, but right now there is little for the tourist to see. 10k/6m to the east is a site on the way to San Marcos known as **La Sabana** (also called Ciudad Perdida) where there are extensive ruins of the remains of buildings and many small mounds where clay heads and figurines have been found. Tripod pottery was also known. The site was settled by the *Tlahuicas*. On the rocky crags nearby there are some petroglyphs and paintings.

It is strongly advisable not to go exploring on your own in this region of Mexico, especially in "off-the-beaten-path" areas. People involved in the narcotics trade use this area of Mexico precisely because it is so isolated and poorly policed. The main highways and cities are generally safe.

In Acapulco itself, visit the museum (9–2, 5–8) in the Instituto Guerrense on the Avenida Costanera Miguel Alemán 4834 which has pottery dating to 2500 B.C.

Route 8: Mexico City to Guadalajara

There are two major routes from Mexico City to Guadalajara. The northern route, via Querétaro and Irapuato (572k/355m) is shorter, faster and easier driving than the southern route via Toluca and Morelia (672k/417m). The southern route is much more scenic, especially just east of Morelia where the road snakes through the pine-forested mountains for miles. Archaeologically, the northern route offers the site of **Tula** and the museums in Querétaro, Pueblito and Ocotlán. On the southern route it is possible to visit **Calixtlahuaca**, **Tenango**, **Malinalco** and **Tzintzuntzan** by making side trips from the main route, as well as museums in Toluca, Morelia, Zacapu and Octolán. Several of these sites can be visited in one-day trips from Mexico City (see Route 5-C). Buses leave from both the west (Autobuses de Occidente) and north (Tres Estrellas, Estrella Blanca, La Piedad) terminals in Mexico City.

8-A: VIA QUERÉTARO

Leaving Mexico City, take highway 57D, the toll road to Querétaro. It is about 75k/47m to the Tepeji del Río turnoff. This road will take you through Tepeji and on to **Tula**. The ruins are on a hill overlooking the town. As you approach the top of the hill, take the paved road to the left to the ruins. Further on, if you have time, you can visit the small museum in San Juan del Río or even make the long side trip to **Ranas y Toluquilla**. For directions/descriptions of these places see Route 4-A.

When you get to Querétaro, turn off at the first exit marked "Centro." This will take you onto a street which continues as Corregidora after you cross Zaragoza going north. This goes directly to the main plaza. There is a church on the corner, and next to it the Regional Museum (Tue–Sat, 10–4:00; Adm.). The Pre-Columbian collection is not large, but it is interesting because it is typical of this part of Mexico and has a number of *Tarascan* pieces.

At the west end of town, if you take the free highway 45 instead of the toll road (45D) you will pass the Villa del Pueblito (8k/5m). The road from the highway will take you 3k to the main plaza at the first stop light. Turn right down the narrow street and go one block. The pink building on the corner (the transversal street is Sebastián Gallegos) is the Casa de la Cultura. There is a small museum here, open daily from 5–8 p.m. Continue ahead down the cobblestone road for 3k to the archaeological zone

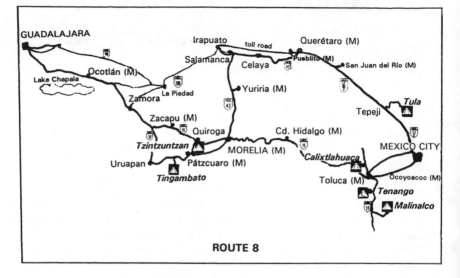

ROUTE 8

called **El Cerrito**. It is enclosed by a cyclone fence and the gate has a padlocked chain, but the trapazoidal mound is clearly visible. The visiting hours on the gate sign have been scratched out. Much of what is in the Querétaro museum came from this center.

As you continue west, just past k 18 you will come to a dirt road (left) leading to the town of San Bartolo (3k). If you have the time and interest in seeing ruins the way archaeologists find them, follow the road through town and 3k farther on at the top of a hill you will see a group of three mounds to your left and a single one off to the right. These are ruins in their pristine state! The mounds are on the list of sites "to be investigated." This may have been a *Toltec* or even a *Tarascan* center. Close to the road are the remains of a once formidable hacienda house, complete with tower, destroyed by the revolutionists between 1910 and 1920.*

Highway 45 will take you to Salamanca where highway 43 runs south to connect with route 8-B. This is one way to combine the archaeological sites of both routes. If you do take highway 43, the museum in the huge ex-Augustinian convent in Yuriria has archaeological pieces from around this area (Tue–Sun, 10–2, 3–4:30; Adm). If you continue on the present route to Guadalajara via highway 110/90 from Irapuato, you will pass through La Piedad. Shortly after, highway 90 goes north, and highway 15 continues ahead to Ocotlán. Here, on Hidalgo street in the center of town, there is a small local museum of two rooms with clay and stone artifacts from the city itself, and Lake Chapala.

For the archaeological sites in and around Guadalajara see Route 11.

* Thanks to Virgil Utter of Modesto, CA for telling me about this site.

8-B: VIA MORELIA

There are two highways, 15 and 134, from Mexico City to Toluca, both the same distance. Highway 134, less traveled, will take you past the Naucalpan district and the area of Tlatilco where much Pre-Columbian material dating from a farming center around 800 B.C. was found and is now on display in the National Museum. However, there is a one-room museum in the town itself on Vía Gustavo Boz 200. Highway 15 passes a short detour to Ocoyoacac (left). On Callejón de la Cruz the Casa de la Cultura has the Mora Museum which features the archaeology and ethnology of the *Matlazincas* and *Aztecs* who inhabited this part of Mexico. Both highways meet highway 55 which goes north 12k/7m to a paved road (left) which will take you to **Calixtlahuaca**, two kilometers from the highway. Go through the village, and a road (left) goes a few hundred meters to the parking area. You will have to do some climbing in order to see everything (8–6; Adm).

Calixtlahuaca (kah-leesht-lah-wah'-kah) means "houses on the plain" which borders the Tejalpa river, although the main structure is on a hill called Tenismó which has a long, gentle slope. The most important excavations and studies have been made by J. García Payón, starting in 1931. This was the center of the *Matlazincas* who settled in the Toluca valley after coming from the north, possibly from **Chicomoztoc**, although there is some evidence that it may have been settled as early as 1700 B.C. and some archaeologists see *Huastec* influences and traces of **Teotihuacán** and *Toltec* culture. After Axayácatl conquered it in 1474, it became an *Aztec* outpost against the *Tarascans*, but Moctezuma II destroyed it in 1510 after an attempted revolt. The main temple, a round structure in four tiers, was dedicated to Ehécatl, the wind god (the statue is now in the Mexico City museum). It was reconstructed four times and is now 12 meters tall and 22 in diameter. On a higher hill is the temple to the rain god, one of several structures around a plaza. The platform is 20 × 27 meters, and the structure is 19 × 17 meters, and is 12 meters high. The cruciform building was covered with 469 stone skull decorations. Stone pegs on its side indicate that real skulls of sacrificial victims might have been placed there. There is a ball court, and one complex of houses. At the base of the hill is the "calmecac" or priests' quarters which also served as a center of instruction for priestly candidates. This complex was added to several times to form a conglomerate of stepped platforms and units of small rooms, and measure 40 × 28 meters. Pottery from the site is kept in the museum in Toluca.

Once you reach highway 55, instead of going north to **Calixtlahuaca** you can make a side trip south on the same highway to the town of Tenango. The narrow street through town will take you to a paved road which goes up a hill to the very fine site of **Teotenango**. Work began here in 1975 and much has already been restored. It is well worth a visit. Farther south on 55 you come to Tenancingo. A road east from here 20k/13m goes to **Malinalco**, the *Aztec* temple hewn from live rock on a mountain top. For details on these two sites see Route 5-C4.

A stopover in Toluca will make it possible to visit all three sites, as well as the new museum complex in the Centro Cultural Mexiquense 10k/6m from town going west on Av. J. M. Morelos. The Anthropological and Historical museum is at the far end of the complex (Tue–Sun, 10–6; Adm). Here, most of the artifacts from **Calixtlahuaca** are kept.

Highway 15 continues to Morelia. Here, we must pause and say something about the state of Michoacán and the Pre-Columbian people who lived there.

The náhuatl word "michuacan" means "place of the fishermen." The state is, in fact, full of lakes and rivers. Of these, Lake Pátzcuaro is undoubtedly the best known, principally because of the famous "butterfly nets" which the fishermen use. At the same time, there are vast stretches of this state which are practically uninhabited due to the extremely rugged mountain terrain. This likewise makes it difficult to find or reach some of the archaeological sites. Most of the work that has been done has been concentrated in the northeastern part of the state, specifically in and around Pátzcuaro. The first scientific excavations carried out took place in the 1930's, directed by Alfonso Caso and Eduardo Noguera. A few monographs have been written, and some radiocarbon dates obtained, but there is still no reliable chronological sequence established. Sixty-eight sites have been located in the Río Balsas delta, and some work was done there in 1966–67 by the National Institute of Anthropology and History as salvage archaeology when the Solís Dam was constructed. The waters inundated the Infernillo site which pre-dated 500 B.C. No earlier site has been discovered, but some pottery found in a context placing it at 2800 B.C. is among the oldest discovered in Mesoamerica.

The people who inhabited Michoacán were a Nahua-speaking group known as Purepechas. They later mixed with other groups and became known as *Tarascans*. The origins of this group begin around 300 A.D. with the formation of social units in **El Opeño** near Lake Chapala in Jalisco, and in Apatzingan in southern Michoacán. The unification of these groups was a long process which came to a head with the founding of Pátzcuaro on the lake of that name by the Tarascan leader Curátemi some time in the twelfth century. Around this same time a Yanaceo *Chichimec* group joined the Tarascans, bringing with them their warlike character. Two other important centers, **Tzintzuntzan** and Ihautzio were established around Lake

Pátzcuaro. Before king Tariácuri died in the fourteenth century, he divided the empire three ways, giving Pátzcuaro to his son, and Tzintzuntzan and Ihauatzio to his two nephews. Eventually Tzintzuntzan became the capital of the Tarascan empire and at the time of the Spanish conquest it was a thriving city.

The Tarascan ruler Tzitzi undertook the expansion of the empire around 1370 and it eventually included most of present-day Michoacán and parts of Guerrero and Jalisco. This dominion was defended by a chain of forts made of wood, manned by ten thousand soldiers armed with bows and arrows, clubs with obsidian blades, maces, slings and lances who fought in squadrons and used such tactics as surprise attacks. Because of them, the Aztecs were not able to include the Tarascan dominions into their own empire.

The Tarascans were fine artisans, especially in wood, copper, feathers and stone. The women were excellent weavers and were known particularly for their intricate designs. Pottery was mainly brilliantly colored polychrome with stirrup handles and negative painting. Cultural traits included cranial deformation, dental mutilation and depilation of the body, and the wearing of ear and lip plugs. Finds in isolated burials, often in shaft-tombs like those at **El Opeño** show that there were outside influences, particularly in the northern part of the state. In 1528 the Spaniards under Nuño de Guzmán arrived and defeated Tangaxoan, the last of the Tarascan rulers. By 1540 Bishop Vasco de Quiroga was in Pátzcuaro and the acculturation process was well under way. The Tarascan descendents continue many of the old customs. Among their interesting features are their numerous dances many of which still exist and are used, that of the "Old Men" being one of the most popular.

47k/29m after Zitácuaro you come to Ciudad Hidalgo. In town at Cuauhtémoc and Melchor Ocampo streets there is the Taximaroa Museum with a collection of *Tarascan* ceramics.

In Morelia, the Museo Michoacano (mee-cho-ah-kah'-no) also has a collection of *Tarascan* art and artifacts in one of its five "galleries." It is located on 305 Allende, next to the court house opposite the southwest corner of the main plaza. (Tue–Sun, 9–2, 5–7; Adm). Another museum in the Casa de la Cultura (Morelos Norte 480) has over 3,000 pieces and a fantastic collection of masks from all over Mexico. The State Museum located on the corner of Santiago Tapia and Guillermo Prieto also displays *Tarascan* archaeology and ethnology (Tue–Sat, 9–7).

42k/26m west of Morelia you come to Quiroga, and the road south to Pátzcuaro. 10k/6m along this highway you will come to the village of **Tzintzuntzan**. At the south end of town a road to the left will take you up a hill to a spacious and shady parking area, and the temple structures.

Tzintzuntzan (seen-soon'-sahn: 10–5; Adm.) means "place of the humming bird" and once upon a time there were over 250 species here. H. Moedano worked here in 1941, and Rubín de la Borbolla in 1944. More work was done by Piña Chan in the 1960's. The city was founded by the *Tarascans* and Yanaceo *Chichimecs* who had joined a couple of centuries before (see explanation above). The important ruins are on the hill called Yahuarato, where a great plaza was laid out, surrounded by palaces with interior patios, and on the lake side an enormous artificial terrace or platform 440 × 26 meters was built. On top of this seven temple platforms were built, combining rectangular and semicircular forms, each with a small circular temple. These structures are known as "yácatas" (yah'-kah-tahs). They were faced with large slabs of volcanic rock and in some cases engraved with figures and hieroglyphs. These temples were to the gods of the sun, the moon, the earth, fire, vegetation and birth. The dead of the noble class were interred at the base of the circular part, often with their servants and other personages. Grave objects included gold, silver, and copper ornaments, turquoise mosaics, obsidian earrings, featherwork and lacquer ware. Other structures in the area include the priest's house, the Eagle House, and a warehouse. The present church stands where the palace was located. At the time of the Spanish conquest the city had around 40,000 inhabitants.

From the lakefront in Pátzcuaro, it is possible to take a ferry boat to the island of Janitzio (every half hour) where the people still preserve many Pre-Columbian customs including the use of the "butterfly nets." If you can hire a boat and pilot (expensive!) it is a twenty-minute ride to **Ihuatzio** where there are pyramids to the sun and moon, and a Pre-Columbian fortress called Queréndaro (kay-ren'-dah-row). There are also buses from the second class terminal to the towns around the lake; somewhat infrequent and very crowded.

You can return to highway 15 at Quiroga, or take the slightly longer route west from Pátzcuaro to Uruapan and north on highway 37 for 75k/47m to highway 15 to continue west to Zamora. If you do head for Uruapan, about 23k/14.5m west of Pátzcuaro on highway 120 a road (left) will take you to **Tingambato**, a site of *Tarascan* ruins where much **Teotihuacán** influence is evident. An interesting sidelight of this trip is being able to see the volcano Paricutín which grew from a corn field in 1943. If you skip the Pátzcuaro detour, Zacapu is the next town after Quiroga on highway 15. The museum in the city hall on the main plaza has some archaeological pieces. From Zamora there is a choice of highways—one along the north shore of Lake Chapala, and the other on the south side. The northern route goes through Ocotlán where there is a two-room museum on Hidalgo street in the center of town.

For archaeological sites in and around Guadalajara see Route 11.

Route 9: El Paso/Ciudad Juárez to Guadalajara

The basic highway for most of this route is highway 45 which goes through Chihuahua, Durango and Zacatecas. An alternate portion of the route, highway 49, goes through Torreón to Zacatecas. This route is 160k/100m shorter. Taking either route you can visit the two unique and intriguing archaeological sites of **Casas Grandes** and **Chicomoztoc**, and museums in Chihuahua and Zacatecas. The regular route offers possibilities of searching for **Chalchihuites**; the alternate route offers a museum in Torreón. From Ciudad Juárez there are buses to all of the major towns along this route and even to out-of-the-way Casas Grandes. "Chihuahuenses" and "Omnibus de México" also go to Mexico City.

Much of this route is through the hot, barren Chihuahua desert which has miles and miles (and even more kilometers!) of rolling hills, rocks, scrub grass and cacti. Yet this was an important Pre-Columbian area of Mexico. Archaeological finds to date show that structures and artifacts in this part of Mexico bear a striking resemblance to those found in the southwestern United States, pointing out the pattern of migration of people perhaps thousands of years ago. Explorations in 1989 directed by two archaeologists from Oklahoma produced information on 84 locations with some evidence of Pre-Hispanic populations in four somewhat scattered areas of this immense desert. To the west of the route we are considering there is a solid range of mountains where water and vegetation are abundant. Many caves showing evidence of Pre-Columbian habitation have been found, but they are in regions so remote as to be virtually inaccessible, and there are no roads through this area, one of the continent's last untamed wildernesses.

In the northern part of the state many of the inhabitants are descendents of the early settlers and are known as *Tarahumaras*. They still follow some of the ancient customs, including living in rock shelters. This is one of Mexico's indigenous groups which has remained somewhat isolated from the mainstream of Hispanic/Western culture and when archaeologists enter their territory they become somewhat aggressive. The books of Carlos Castaneda (e.g. *Journey to Ixtlán*) offer insights into the people and their culture, and perhaps indirectly into their Pre-Columbian past.

Before you leave Ciudad Juárez, however, visit the fine museum on Av. Paseo de la Independencia at Niños Héroes. It features the western

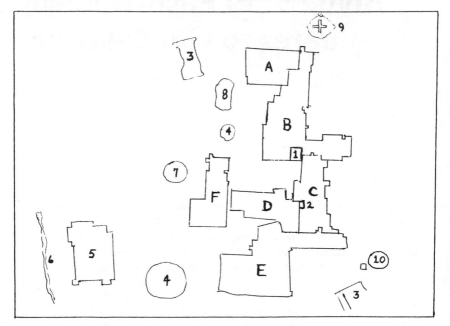

CASAS GRANDES

A housing unit 6
B the well housing unit
C the skulls housing unit
D the dead housing unit
E the pillars housing unit
F the macaw housing unit
I. steam bath
2. watch tower

3. ball courts
4. water storage
5. house of the serpent
6. serpent mound
7. hero's mound
8. mount of the offerings
9. mound of the cross
10. temple

cultures of Mexico—a good overall view, especially if you do not intend to go to those areas.

9-A: VIA HIDALGO DEL PARRAL AND DURANGO (1695K/1055M)

To visit the archaeological site of **Casas Grandes**, turn west on highway 2 about 16k/10m south of Ciudad Juárez (you will already have passed highway 2 going east). Follow 2 west and south. At Janos it becomes highway 10. Continue southeast to Nuevo Casas Grandes. Don't turn into town (left) but stay on the same road until you see another paved road (right) with the sign "Colonia Juárez." 13k/8m along this road you will see a sign indicating the entrance to the archaeological zone. This side trip will add 259k/162m to your total journey, but it is well worth it. The bus line "Chihuahuenses" will take you as far as Nuevo Casas Grandes from the border. Here you can get a local bus to the main plaza of Casas Grandes. A fifteen-minute hike will get you to the ruins.

Casas Grandes (kah'-sahs grahn'-des) was known in former times as Paquimé. The actual Spanish name refers to the numerous and large adobe houses which covered this area. Most of the important archaeological work here was done by the Amerind Foundation under C. C. di Peso in 1961 and 1966, and by the National Institute of Anthropology and History in the early 1970's. The ruins cover an area of 20 hectares, or two square kilometers. This center thrived between 800 and 1300 A.D. and seems to have been a kind of "melting pot" of cultures from southwestern U.S. (the Mogollón group) and Mesoamerica. Thirty-one different entities have been identified and include six communal adobe house complexes, some five stories tall, with stairways, windows, and in some cases built-in fireplaces, 3 ball courts, water tanks, ovens, circular religious centers and one which was probably related to astronomy, an irrigation system, platform mounds, a truncated pyramid and a turkey corral. Burials under houses have revealed beautiful basket work, pottery, pipes, shell and turquoise mosaic work, copper bells and a variety of everyday tools. Other tombs are scattered over a wide area. Most are of stone blocks in an elliptical form about a meter and a half long. However, some skeletons have been found of persons about 1.80 meters tall. Pottery is mainly black on white, occasionally with red lines, and with geometric designs. The mud walls have eroded with time but there is still much to see. The city was sacked and burned by nomadic Indians in 1340.

From Nuevo Casas Grandes highway 10 goes east and joins highway 45 coming south from Ciudad Juárez. This takes you to Chihuahua. To go to the Regional Museum stay on Universidad which becomes Carranza. A few blocks farther on you will come to Allende. Turn right, go one block and turn left onto Bolívar. The museum is on Bolívar one block after you cross Independencia and pass a small park. It is located in a pink stucco house built in the nineteenth-century French style (Tues.–Sun., 10–1; 4–7; Adm.). This should not be confused with the Quinta Luz which was Pancho Villa's house and has also been turned into a museum. The Cultural Center on Aldama 430 at Ocampo street has a beautiful collection of polychrome vases from **Casas Grandes**.

South of Chihuahua highway 45 turns west at Jiménez and goes to Hildalgo del Parral (where Pancho Villa was assassinated) and then south. The whole area north of Durango and that to the southeast is full of caves and Pre-Columbian sites, but not enough archaeological work has been done. This was a Zape Indian center and there is evidence of a whole chain of villages which stretch along the mountain river valleys down to **Chicomoztoc**. In Durango, there is a museum of Anthropology and History on 100 South Victoria street with a small display of archaeological and ethnological artifacts (Tue–Sat, 10–1; 3–6; Sun 11–5; Adm).

One of the mountain fortress cities mentioned above is **Chalchihuites**. The site can be reached from Sombrerete on highway 45 southeast of Durango. From here it is 35k/22m to the town on a gravel and dirt road that is frequently in poor condition. The ruins themselves are 6k west of town. A jeep or pickup truck could manage fairly well.

Chalchihuites (chahl-chee-wee'-tes) means "precious stones." This important center was studied by M. Gamio in 1910 and by E. Noguera in 1930 and again in 1960. It is one of a chain of hilltop cities and fortresses and the northern edge of Mesoamerica, the most impressive of which is **Chicomoztoc**. Different cultural phases have been identified, ranging from 500 to 950 A.D., but the center was providing **Teotihuacán** with metal ores already in 300 A.D. There are four major groups of constructions known as Moctezuma, El Chapín, Alta Vista and El Pedregoso. This mud and stone city was built around a series of central courts surrounded by platforms for houses and other structures. The longest one measures 36.5 meters on each side. One building, covering 400 square meters, has four rows of 28 columns made of adobe brick and covered by baked mud. They are about 2.80 meters thick. The whole unit forms a maze of rooms and patios with passageways for communication. The complex is strikingly similar to several sites in the U.S. southwest. The multi-form pottery found is *Tarascan* in design and generally decorated with red on cream in both geometric and zoomorphic forms. Another type is black polished ware, incised with animals or geometric forms filled with red paint.

Highway 45 continues on to Fresnillo and Zacatecas where it meets highway 54 which goes on to Guadalajara. If you go into Zacatecas, there is a Pre-Columbian collection in the Pedro Coronel museum next to Santo Domingo church on Fernando Villapando street (a block northwest of the main plaza: 10–2, 4–7; Adm. Closed Thursday). 40k/25m from the junction you will see the archaeological zone sign and a paved road to the left. It will take you to the ruins of **Chicomoztoc** (also known as La Quemada) which can be seen from the highway, sprawling over the hilltop. The ruins are impressive and fascinating (Tue–Sat, 10–5, Adm).

Chicomoztoc (chee-ko-mo'-stalk) means "seven caves." C. de Berghes drew a plan of these formidable ruins in 1833. I. Marquina, P. Armillas and García Vega studied and reported on the site in 1951 and 1952. Excavations and restoration work took place in 1987–88 under Peter Jiménez, partly with the help of New York State University at Buffalo, aided by the National Science Foundation. This center, possibly the ancient Zacatlán, and once called Tuitlán, is thought to be the origin of several groups which moved south to the Anáhuac valley, including the Nahuas, Tepenacs, Acolhuas and Chalcas. Mythology and legend say that the first men came from the interior of the earth from which the seven caves served as the exit. There are, in fact, several caves in the surrounding hills.

The area was occupied around a thousand years and reached a high point between 900 and 1000 A.D. The city probably collapsed after **Tula** did (1168), and in fact tribes moving from here may have brought about the downfall of the *Toltec* capital. Even *Zapotec* myths give the "seven caves" as the place of their origin, and *Otomí* expansion probably began here.

The ruins show remarkable resemblance to many of the southwestern U.S., but they also have Mesoamerican characteristics. Situated on a hill some 185 meters high, this city had only one entrance up a narrow path and through two structures (one is reminded of entering the Acropolis in Athens). There are three main groups to these ruins: two inside of the "fortress" on the hill, and one on the lower slopes. The main structure on the lower slope may have been a ceremonial center, or a gathering place for the governing council. The 11 cylindrical columns are 5 meters high; the walls are 2.60 meters thick. The structures on the hill made of "tabular" stone, are a unique architectural feature. The unusual small pyramid inside (called a Votive Pyramid) was restored in 1955. All in all, the site is the work of skilled laborers and was certainly not built by "barbaric nomads."

The remainder of the trip is mainly through mountain valleys. At times the scenery is really splendid. Highway 54 will take you right into the city of Guadalajara. For archaeological sites in and around the city see Route 11.

9-B: VIA TORREÓN (1535K/954M)

This route is the same as 9-A as far as Jiménez. Here you continue south on highway 49 instead of turning west. You do not have to go into or through Torreón, but there is a Regional Museum with three rooms dedicated to archaeology of the area, and some Pre-Columbian objects found in and near the caves in the hills of Coahuila and other parts of Mexico. It is located on east Juárez street in Venustiano Carranza park.

Highway 49 will join highway 45 just north of Fresnillo and this in turn joins highway 54 near Zacatecas. The rest of the trip is the same as Route 9-A.

Route 10: The Western Border Towns to Guadalajara

There is only one north-south artery, highway 15, between the western U.S. border towns and Guadalajara. Unfortunately, there is only one major site on this route, **Los Toriles** near Ixtlán del Río, about halfway between Tepic and Guadalajara. Secondary sites include La Pintada (petroglyphs), **Amapa**, **Sentispac** and **Etzatlán**. Hermosillo and Tepic have good museums, and there are several others in smaller towns. From the western Mexican border towns there are buses to all of the cities along this route, and even on to Mexico City ("Transportes Norte Sonora" and "Tres Estrellas" from Tecate, Mexicalli and Tijuana; "Transportes del Pacifico" from Nogales).

From California and Arizona there are six major crossing points. All of them connect into Mexico's east-west highway 2, which junctions at the town of Santa Ana with the north-south highway 15 which begins at Nogales. From Santa Ana it is 1606k/999m to Guadalajara. The first 700k/437m (or more, depending on where you enter Mexico) are through the state of Sonora.

This state is largely a desert of cacti and thorny scrub, separated by isolated mountain ranges, although in the northeast there are high, grassy plains (4,000–7,000 ft.). Since the 1920's there have been sporadic surveys and archaeological investigations, but only a few excavations, and those on a rather small scale.

What has been found shows that the people who lived in this area were influenced by the Hohokam and Mogollon cultures of the southwestern United States. Shell mounds on the coast, and stone tools associated with them, show that there may have been big-game hunters here as early as 9,000 B.C. Inhabitants of the northeastern section moved from caves to temporary camps to small villages between 500 and 1400 A.D. Simultaneously, in the northwest, terraces and houses were being made at Trincheras between 800 and 1100. Sixteen mounds at La Playa still need to be excavated and studied. The pottery which has been found is a unique purple-on-red.

The southern area is the least known, but red ware dating from

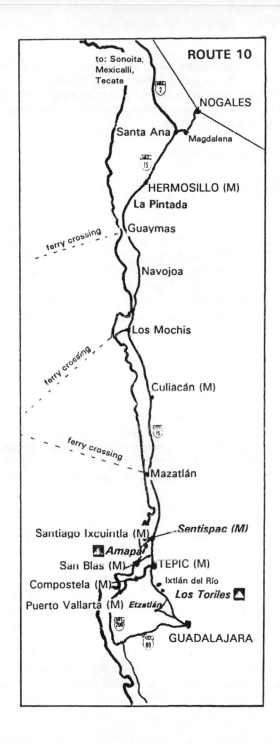

around 1100 has been found in the Huatabampo area. It is here, and along the coast to the north, that the *Yaqui* Indians lived. They rebelled not only against the Spaniards, but also against the Mexican government. Another related group, the *Mayo*, also developed in this same geographical region.

If you enter Mexico through the San Isidro/Tijuana, the Calexico/ Mexicali, the San Luis Río Colorado or the Lukeville/Sonoita crossings, between Sonoita and Santa Ana you will pass through Caborca and Altar, old settlements which are on the official list of archaeological sites. This whole region is called the Altar Desert, and the name is suggestive. Eventually the known ruins of La Playa and Trincheros may have side roads to them. Investigations made in 1983 show that the region has been continuously inhabited since the late Pleistocene period. In Mexicalli at 120 Alvaro Obregón the city museum has a room dedicated to archaeology.

Highway 15 from Nogales to Santa Ana takes you through Magdalena. If you have time, stop at the main plaza and see the special monument to the great Jesuit missionary of Sonora and Arizona, Father Eusebio Kino. It is unique. If you look through the window, you can see the saintly man's skeleton where archaeologists found it when they were digging for traces of the old colonial church and the verification of the missionary's believed grave site. (If you came from the west, it is a 17k/11m detour northeast).

Continuing south, as you enter Hermosillo you will come to a circle with a statue of Fr. Kino. This street curves south and blends into Rodríguez Boulevard. As this avenue makes another bend left you will pass a park. The building across the street to your left is the Museum of the University of Sonora. The displays of very early Pre-Columbian techniques in shell and stone are especially interesting (Wed–Sat, 10–5:30; Sun 10–3:30; Adm). There is a Regional Museum in the former penitentiary at the intersection of California and Jesús García streets which also has a Pre-Columbian section.

If you stay on the boulevard, it will take you out of town and continue as highway 15. About 64k/40m south of Hermosillo, you will see a sign indicating La Pintada, and a small restaurant across the road. Toward the back of the restaurant there is a dirt road which goes through a large fence opening. It can be driven only in the dry season, and though full of ruts and bumps is passable. It will take you about three kilometers to some rock formations where there are petroglyphs. There are plans for turning this area into a state park.

Farther south, as you enter the city of Guaymas, you will see a large hill to your left. Pre-Columbian tombs were found here and probably were from the *Yaqui* Indians, whose descendents can still be found in the vicinity. However, archaeology is definitely over-shadowed by sports fishing here! A ferry boat from here goes to Santa Rosalía on Route 12 once a day (11 a.m.) four days a week.

Continuing on, near Navojoa you come to *Mayo* Indian country and you will notice the differences in the physical features of these people from those you saw in the north. Again, the villages to the west offer anthropological insights to earlier times and present-day Indian customs. Huatabampo is listed with the Mexican archaeological sites, but no Pre-Columbian ruins are in evidence.

81k/52m south of Navojoa you leave the immense state of Sonora and pass to the Pacific coastal state of Sinaloa. There are a lot of villages in the mountains east of here and some of them certainly have Pre-Columbian origins.

Much of what is known about the archaeology of this long, coastal state is by way of analogy, comparing the few finds that have been made with similar cultures of other areas. From this it would appear that the cultures of Sinaloa are linked more closely to central Mexico than they are to the southwestern United States, though some have argued for direct migration and its influences. While a number of sites have been identified (63 in the Culiacán area in 1935, and 34 along the southern coast, for instance), no pre-classic site has yet been discovered, nor any major urban center of stone architecture, nor any monumental sculpture.

The Guasave-Huatabampo area was occupied between 700 and 1000 A.D., and G. Ekholm found 166 graves at a Guasave mound in 1938–39. Chametla was a classic site and white slipped ware and polychrome pottery were found here. The best chronology to date is that of the Aztatlán complex, in the Culiacán region. It has been divided into three time slots: 1000–1200, 1200–1350 and 1350 to 1450. Six-color polychrome pottery has been found, along with silver and gold objects. It is possible that a migration around 1300 brought **Cholula**-style pottery to the area, especially the use of the tripod vessel. It seems, also, that after 800 A.D. urn burials became common. Other artifacts of the Sinaloa cultures include bone daggers, obsidian knives, shell and bead bracelets, copper bells and rings, leather shields and the bow and arrow.

There is no evidence that there was any "empire" or domination by one group in this part of Mexico.

156k/96m from Navojoa you come to Los Mochis. The port of To-polobampo is 20k/12m from here. There is a ferry boat from here to La Paz on Route 12 every Monday at 10 a.m.

At Culiacán, the Coltzín Museum on the Malecón Niños Héroes and Dr. Ruperto Paliza contains a good collection of *Mayo* Indian artifacts. The Regional Museum is located on Rafael Buelna and Vicente Guerrero. It displays ceramics from several west coast sites like Guasave and Chametla mentioned above. There are two other things the adventuresome archaeology buff can look for. A dirt road from the east end of town goes 32k/20m to an artificial lake created by the Sanalona dam. There are ruins on the opposite side of this lake, but no road to them. Also, in Ymala, near here, there are petroglyphs carved into the canyon walls. From Mazatlán, the ferry goes daily to La Paz to connect with Route 12.

24k/15m south of Mazatlán you will come to Villa Unión where highway 40 begins and goes east over one of Mexico's most difficult roads to Durango where you can join Route 9-A. Continuing south on highway 15 you will near Acaponeta. When you cross the river, you are in the state of Nayarit, one of much archaeological interest.

A number of Pre-Columbian sites have been discovered in this small western state. Many of them are along the Pacific shore in the form of shell middens. Another evidence of early habitation are the petroglyphs which have been found near Huajicori and San Juan Peyotán in Boquillas canyon, at El Tambor and in the vicinity of Compostela.

As is the case with most of the western cultures, we know Nayarit best through its pottery forms. The pre-classic period is characterized by undecorated flat-bottomed plates of brown, sandy clay. There are also stirrup-handled vases of reddish clay, decorated with white, dotted lines. Ceramic human figures have large thighs, stumpy feet, thin arms, a well-shaped nose, "coffee bean" eyes, and wear ear and nose rings. Sometimes they are depicted as kneeling with their arms crossed. Most of the pottery has been found in bottle-shaped tombs which were covered with a stone slab.

In the formative period, ceramic "scenes" of multiple persons (up to twenty) were made. Frequently they are dancers. There are also scenes of the ball game and the ball court. This ceramic style continued in the classic period, but the figurines included dogs, warriors, musicians and stooped old men (often with a hare lip). The Teotihuacán influence was felt even at this great distance. The *Cora* culture (still existing) had its origins here, and **Amapa**, Cajititlán, **Ixtlán del Río**, La Yesca, Mexcaltitlán and Santiago Ixcuintla became important centers. The people in this mountainous country mastered terrace cultivation. Pottery forms included concave dishes of brown, polished clay with geometric designs in white, red or cream; tripod pottery with hollow legs that rattled; clay figurines, such as those described above, but with fresco paintings on them. The artisans were equally adept at working gold or silver into sheets from which they made hawksbells, filigree figures and nose rings. Some vessels were formed from marble and there were pectorals of jade beads.

Most of these finds came from shaft tombs, some of them twenty meters deep which had mortuary chambers on both sides about three meters in diameter. The openings to the shafts are about two and a half feet wide.

75k/47m from Acaponeta there is a side road (right) to Santiago Ixcuintla. There is a museum in the city hall (Mon–Fri, 9–3; 5–7). You go through this village and some 8k/5m farther, on the left side of the road, are the ruins of **Amapa** (ah-mah'-pah).

This site was studied by the U.C.L.A. field team in 1959. D. M. Pendergast examined it further in 1960–62, and J. B. Mountjoy in 1969. Excavations show that there were three stages of occupation: 250–750 A.D., 700–900 and 900–1520. Around 900 this was an active metal working center (gilded copper) and perhaps an important trade center, given its proximity to the sea. There are some 200 mounds in an area covering one and a half square kilometers. Excavations have brought to light houses, a ceremonial center, and a ball court. A cemetery has yielded 800 pieces of pottery of forty different types, along with carved stone heads, figurines, spindle whorls, copper objects and fishhooks, axes, awls, pins, ear spools, etc. Pottery is mainly of orange and red-rimmed ware, showing intricate, stylistic variety.

A little farther on a road goes to **Sentispac**. Some claim these ruins are of the first pyramids built in Mexico. There is a local museum (9–3; 5–7). Still farther south on highway 15, the port of San Blas has dozens of archaeological sites, most of them shell middens from very early seacoast cultures. You might find one yourself if you explore the beaches. A site known as Chacalilla lies 10k/6m south of the port. If you like historical archaeology, you can see the ruins of the old Spanish ship-building town that once existed here. The city hall of San Blas has a museum open Mon–Fri, 9–3; 5–7.

Tepic, the capital of Nayarit, is the next stop. There is a good museum here. To get to it follow the highway to Mexico Street (it is marked as highway 200 to your right). Turn left into town. The museum will be on your left, about halfway between the state capitol building and the main plaza, in a large restored colonial building on the corner of Zapata street. Much of what has been found in this area, including some statues, is on display in this museum.

If you detour from highway 15, a road from Tepic takes you to Compostela. In the city hall there are two rooms of clay figurines reflecting the daily life of the region between 200 and 800 A.D. Different! From here, a road directly east gets you back to highway 15. Or, you can continue south toward Puerto Vallarta. On Isla del Coale there is a small museum which features western Mexico but has reproductions from other cultures also. There is no road back except the one you came on, which makes this a long detour. You could continue south on 200 until it meets highway 80 and go north to Guadalajara. This way you could see **Barra de Navidad** and **Autlán** (see Route 11-C).

81k/57m east of Tepic you will come to the town of Ixtlán. Once again, the city hall has a museum (9–3; 5–7) of some importance because of the nearby ruins. Three kilometers on the other side of the town in the midst of lush green vegetation you will see the familiar sign indicating an archaeological zone. To your left is a dirt road which crosses some railroad tracks, dips down into a culvert and continues up the incline on the other side. The total distance is perhaps thirty meters. About one hundred meters farther on you will see the ruins of **Los Toriles**. The circular temple stands out right away. Other ruins are scattered around the general vicinity. Be careful as you walk around. The stone is lava and sometimes the rugged edges are sharp.

Los Toriles (lows tow-ree'-less) was discovered by the parish priest, Fr. Navarro, in 1899. Archaeologists C. Lumholtz (1902), E. W. Gifford (1950) and I. Contreras (1966) worked here, and excavations are presently being done by R. Arana. The site has indications of having been a religious center, but the ceramics are largely utilitarian and contrary to most other sites the nude figure predominates in the large, hollow figurines (70 to 80 centimeters) which are both monochrome and polychrome. The most striking monument is the circular structure 4 meters high and 30 meters in diameter. The two small platforms within the structure served as bases for two temples. (One source says they were the sacrificial altars.) J. Corona calls this the temple of Quetzalcoatl. Several other platform structures in the area presumably had dwellings and possibly other temples on them. Some burials have been found in the area, in the stepped shaft graves like those found at **El Opeño**. Ixtlán del Río seems to have been at its height between 900 and 1250 A.D.

A short distance after you leave Ixtlán, you will cross into the state of Jalisco (change your watch at this point to Central Standard Time).

As is the case with the other states of western Mexico, the Pre-Columbian sites are for the most part tucked away in the mountain regions, and not easily accessible. Enough has been found, however, to give a general picture of the early cultures and their development.

Petroglyphs and rock art from a very early period have been found near V. Carranza, Ciudad Guzmán, Puerto Vallarta, El Tuito and Ajijic on Lake Chapala. Caves along the Bolaños river indicate early habitation. The pre-classic period is characterized by several kinds of ceramic styles: a spheroid, short-necked pottery of reddish or light brown clay; flat-bottomed ceremonial bowls with a human effigy near the base; some animal shapes; figurines in human form with "coffee bean" eyes (like those of Colima), and heart-shaped mouths, wearing a kind of short apron or tunic.

During the classic period there were several important centers, including **Ixtépete** in the Atemayac valley, the location of present-day Guadalajara, and **Autlán**, El Arenal, Tuxcacuesco and Sayula to the south. The pottery of this period varies from brown, globular shapes or spheroid types with a bowl neck decorated in bands of vertical, wavy or horizontal lines to tripod, polychromed types with intricate designs. Ceramic figures depict men and women (sometimes aged) with elongated heads and a prominent nose; the men, thought to be priests, seated with bowls in their laps and the women in short skirts, their breasts decorated with spirals. Clay boxes were also made—and with exact-fitting lids! There is a range of other artifacts from grinding stones to hammered gold discs.

Most of the finds have come from shaft tombs such as those at **Etzatlán** or **El Opeño**. These people do not seem to have been particularly warlike, and it was probably sheer distance which kept them from falling under the dominion of the *Tarascans* or the *Aztecs*.

There is one other site before you reach Guadalajara, but you will have to go somewhat out of your way to get there. About 62k/40m from Ixtlán you will come to Magdalena. From here, a rather poor road goes 22k/13m south to **Etzatlán** where there are some shaft tombs, all looted long ago. P. T. Furst investigated these in the 1960's. The total contents of one tomb are in the Los Angeles County Museum. There are also structural remains in the area. This spot can also be reached by a paved road which begins 24k/15m west of Guadalajara, but you will have to go back 55k/34m to this village. The ruins are 7k from town on the former San Sebastián hacienda.

For places of interest in and around Guadalajara see Route 11.

Route 11: Around Guadalajara and into Colima

11-A: IN GUADALAJARA AND VICINITY

A1) The Regional Museum in Guadalajara has a superb collection representing the Jalisco, Colima and Nayarit cultures. It occupies the whole block between Independencia and Hidalgo, and between 6 de Diciembre and Pino Suárez (Tues.–Sun., 9–3:45; Adm.). There is another smaller but good archaeological museum on 889 16 de Septiembre, on the west side of Parque Agua Azul at the south end of town (Mon.–Fri., 10–6; Adm.) called the Archaeological Museum of Western Mexico.

A2) Ixtépete is a seldom visited but very accessible site. It is located near the by-pass on the southwest side of the city, not far from La Pirámide Trailer Park or the children's park at Las Fuentes urbanization. From in town, Av. López Mateos is the easiest way to get to the by-pass. Near the trailer park there is a new road. Turn onto it and less than twenty meters from the highway you will see a dirt road to your right. It will take you sixty meters or so to the site.

Ixtépete (eesh-tay'-pay-tay) was excavated and studied in the 1960's by J. Corono Nuñez, R. Piña Chan and C. Sáenz. In recent years work has been done by O. Schöndube. Though relatively little is actually visible now, the ruins probably extend to nearby Cerro del Colli and probably had very early origins. Ixtépete seems to have become a true settlement around 100 A.D. when the first of six superimposed pyramids was built. The platform structure was 16 × 20 meters and 1.83 meters high. Succeeding structures eventually made the base 42 × 38 meters and increased the height to 6 meters. The second pyramid shows **Teotihuacán** influence, and Ixtépete was probably one of the sites which radiated this influence through western Mexico. Teotihuacán type figurines have also been found. Cremation was practiced and burial urns were used, settling this culture apart from the not-too-distant shaft tomb sites of **El Opeño** and **Ezatlán**. After 1000 A.D. the site probably came under *Tarascan* influence and continued until the Spanish conquest.

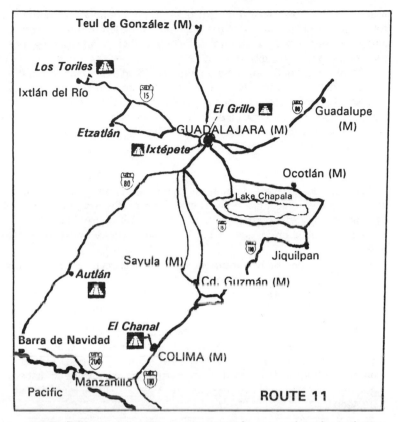

Teul de González (M)

Los Toriles
Ixtlán del Río

El Grillo   Guadalupe
GUADALAJARA (M)   (M)

Etzatlán
Ixtépete

Ocotlán (M)

Lake Chapala

Sayula (M)   Jiquilpan

Autlán   Cd. Guzmán (M)

El Chanal
Barra de Navidad
COLIMA (M)

Manzanillo
Pacific   ROUTE 11

A3) El Grillo (gree'-yo) is a comparatively new archaeological zone. This center came to attention during the building of the by-pass around the city. In fact, the by-pass cuts right through it. From **Ixtépete** follow the by-pass north across highway 15 and keep going north past where Av. Avila Camacho goes toward Zapopan. The road will curve back east, and as you near Zapopan you will see a mound group on the south (right) side of the highway. There are some burial sites on the north side, all looted now. The University of North Carolina excavated at this site, and recent work has been done by L. J. Galván. If ethnology interests you, there is a *Huichol* Indian arts and crafts center in Zapopan which also has a "museum" with it.

11-B: TO THE WEST

If you have not come into Guadalajara on highway 15 from the west, then you might want to visit one or two sites within a day's round trip. 24k/15m west of the city a paved road goes to Ameca. 15k/9m along this road there is a fork. Take the right branch and continue to **Etzatlán**, a total distance of 55k/34m from the highway. Or go left to Ameca. There is a room in the Casa de la Cultura with some 800 clay and stone figurines (one of a woman giving birth).

137k/85m west of Guadalajara on highway 15, in a very beautiful setting on the outskirts of the village of Ixtlán, you can visit the ruins of **Los Toriles**. The archaeological zone sign will indicate a dirt road to the right which crosses railroad tracks, dips into a culvert and runs up the incline on the other side for some thirty meters. The ruins are visible from here.

See Route 10 for information on these sites.

11-C: TO THE SOUTH

C1) The Lake Chapala district has been the scene of archaeological work for quite some time now. There is some digging going on near Chapala itself, and a permanent lab has been set up in Ajijic. The road along the south shore passes two or three other sites where work is also being done.

In Ocotlán there is a two-room museum of artifacts from the town and Lake Chapala. It is on 1 Hidalgo Street.

C2) The ruins of **Autlán** are considered to be of major importance. They lie 188k/118m southwest of Guadalajara via highways 15 and 80.

The town of **Autlán** (out-lahn') existed in Pre-Columbian times. The ruins were studied by I. Kelly in 1939, 1940 and 1942. Shell and clay bracelets, obsidian flints and four types of figurines indicate early habitation in the area. Three ceramic phases have been distinguished, but no metal has been found. A few structural remains can be seen.

C3) For exciting archaeological exploration, follow route C2 above to **Autlán**. Continue on highway 80 for another 107k/67m to **Barra de Navidad** on the Pacific Ocean. This lovely port is fast being overrun by real estate people and tourists, but the Colima Indians were here long before.

Barra de Navidad (bah'-rrah day nah-vee-dahd') was included in the U.C.L.A. Project A study during 1960–62, with V. Lombardo and M. V. Wise investigating. All that remains today is a mound 18 meters in diameter and 8 meters high. Chipped obsidian, stone artifacts and some utilitarian pottery have been found. This was probably a seasonal site used between 650 and 1100 A.D. Other artifacts have been found in the sand around the general area.

One area of the beach, known as Salagua, is said to have been called Tzalahua originally, and was the capital of a Colima tribe. It has been verified that Las Hadas beach is on a Pre-Columbian site, and the section of beach known as **Playa Tesoro** has yielded all kinds of artifacts on the beach itself and in the nearby hillside, even in recent times, and figurines are sometimes still found in the sand dunes.

Playa Tesoro (ply'-yah tay-so'-row) in Spanish means "treasure beach," and was so called because it was thought that treasure would be found where old artifacts had been discovered. This area was also included in the U.C.L.A. Project A. Four kinds of pottery sherds have been identified, and four groups of figurines, with seventeen different types. Most of the pottery is heavy, utility ware. The site has been damaged by construction and by a hurricane which struck the area in 1959. Artifacts, however, still come to light from time to time.

16k/10m southeast from the previously mentioned sites on highway 200 you will cross the Chacala river into the state of Colima.

Because the archaeological sites in this small, mountainous state are so difficult to get to, it is important to give some idea of the general cultural picture as it has been pieced together from the artifacts and sites which have been discovered over the years.

The first settlements in the area date from around 300 B.C. Colima legend says that the first people came from a frog god which had been impregnated by the Milky Way. The centers which were eventually established such as Ortices, Armería, Las Animas, Tecomán, Periquillo, Cajitlán and Colima probably formed some kind of a loose federation. It is unlikely that they were united into a single state. The people did band together to defend themselves against the Spaniards, and twice defeated them. Only with the aid of the *Tarascans* were the Spaniards able to subdue the people of Colima.

The most interesting feature of this culture is the long ceramic tradition which began with figurines depicting varied aspects of life. Dogs were a favorite subject, and they were also buried with the dead since they were supposed to lead the person's spirit into the after life. Along with these and other zoomorphic (animal-shaped) forms, the Colima people made bright orange ceramic figures which were hollow and were distinguished by their "coffee bean" eyes and the black speckled surface. There were also solid figures of dancers, hunchbacks (often wearing pectorals in the form of human heads), women nursing children or grinding corn, musicians with flutes or drums, stone throwers and warriors with trophy heads. Along a different line, there are incense burners in the shape of flower baskets, double-headed snakes, or different deities. Gourd-shaped vessels were made, along with others in the forms of plants, flowers and fruits. Red or brown globular vases, often with snake or bird heads modeled on them, and decorated in black are also characteristic of the Colima cultures. Finally, there are whistles, flutes and ocarinas in ceramic form.

Deep shaft tombs have been found at Cajitlán and burial urns at Ranelio Cuixmala. **El Chanal**, near Colima, is presently under study, and the University of Oklahoma worked with Angel Lara to excavate at Hacienda El Cobano. Hopefully in time a clearer chronology can be established as excavations increase and more comes to light to reveal the cultural traits of the Pre-Columbian people in the southwest corner of Mexico.

Highway 110 begins about 10k/6m after Armería and will take you into Colima.

C4) The Regional Museum in Colima is located in the old Casino Hotel on the main plaza. It has an excellent collection (over 2000 pieces) representing the Pre-Columbian cultures of Colima, with an incredible quantity of fascinating clay figurines (Tue–Sat, 8–7, Sun 8–1). North of here on 27 de Septiembre the Museo de la Máscara y Danza also has Pre-Columbian artifacts.

If you take the highway north to Ciudad Guzmán, between Reforma and Clemente Orozco streets on Dr. Angel González 21 you will find the Archaeological Museum of Western Cultures. The building which housed French nuns in the 17th century now contains artifacts from towns in the region, including a collection of huge urns used for burials.

You can also take highway 54 from Ciudad Guzmán and 28k/17m farther on is Sayula. At Portal Sur 3, in the heart of town, there is a small museum of artifacts basically from the Colima region. Highway 54 joins 80 to take you into Guadalajara. You can also skip Sayula and take the new direct road to highway 80. Another choice is to follow highway 110 north to Jiquilpan and continue north to connect with highway 35 west to Ocotlán to visit the museum on Hidalgo street.

11-D: TO THE NORTH

About 50k/32m north of Guadalajara on the road to Tlatenango there is an archaeological zone 2k from Teul de González. This is reported to have been a religious center of the *Caxcanes*, one of the many *Chichimec* tribes from the north. There is a new Paleontological Museum with fossil remains of various kinds.

Route 12: Baja California

Almost completely isolated geographically from the rest of Mexico, the peninsula of Baja California for a long time was not incorporated fully into the political, economic or cultural life of Mexico. Besides being separated from the mainland by the Sea of Cortés, a mountain range runs down the middle of the peninsula, like a spine, making road building and travel difficult, but helping the area to preserve its primeval look and charm. In spite of this, there has been a fairly continuous chain of chronicles and writings since Spanish occupation and the ethnohistory of the region is pretty well known. Even with the scarcity of archaeological expeditions and undertakings, enough information has come from individuals who have explored archaeological areas and found and identified artifacts to be able to get something of a picture of the past.

Overcoming obstacles of geography and climate, engineers have succeeded in building a fine highway all the way down the peninsula from Tijuana (tee-wah'-nah; not tee-*uh*-wah'-nah) to La Paz, and improving the road from there to San Lucas.

Long thought to be a pretty barren land, the peninsula actually has a number of streamlets and rivers which means it can support animal life. Hunting and fishing are the major attractions to this part of Mexico. These same life-giving and life-sustaining attributes existed long ago, too, and it is not surprising that the archaeological maps of Mexico show a chain of Pre-Columbian sites all through the mountain range where caves undoubtedly provided shelter and defense and where food was plentiful. Along the shores there are clusters of sites where paleolithic and neolithic peoples lived out their simple, rustic lives as they sustained themselves from the riches of the sea. The long-abandoned mission complexes evidence the fact that later on the Spanish friars tried to bring the people together to instruct them in faith and the ways of the civilized world.

The peninsula can be divided archaeologically into three major areas.

In the north, along the border with the United States, and in the area from Tijuana to Ensenada, the *San Dieguito* culture developed in three stages, beginning around 8,000 B.C. All kinds of stone tools have been found, and many shell ornaments. Petroglyphs have also been discovered. With the abundance of sea food and whatever wildlife could be found in the mountains, the inhabitants of this area could have remained for a very long period of time at a purely paleolithic level since they had no real challenges to force them to invent and develop.

The middle third of the peninsula developed what has been called the *Comondú* culture. Metate Cave and Caguama Cave are two of the important sites. San Borjita Cave, near Mugelé, has paintings on the cave walls. This culture is characterized by coiled baskets, flat milling stones, obsidian arrowpoints, gathering hooks and pounding stones. This was evidently a hunting-and-gathering culture, still somewhat nomadic and without pottery or textiles.

The lower third of the peninsula developed the *Las Palmas* culture. Up to 1966 1,181 recorded surface finds had been made in this area. These include tools of all kinds made of stone, dart-throwers, nets, baskets and even human hair capes. As might be expected of a group dwelling on the seashore, paddles were also found. The off-shore islands have burial caves. In these and others of the region, skeletons with long, narrow skulls called dolichrocranial have been found.

In many ways Baja California is an archaeologist's paradise because there is still so much to be done and it has been left unmolested for so long. Now, with the highway completed, some of the caves and Pre-Columbian sites will certainly come to light. Hopefully those who find them will report them so that they may be properly excavated and studied.

The two entry points are Tijuana and Mexicalli. In Tijuana, on Paseo de los Héroes and Mina, there is a small museum in the Regional Cultural Center with some 50 archaeological pieces (Mon-Fri, 11–7; Sat, Sun, 11–8; Adm). In Mexicalli, the city museum at 1209 Alvaro Obregón has a room dedicated to archaeology. Those who come across at Mexicalli have to go west to Tecate and take highway 3 south to join highway 1, since the highway south from Mexicalli (5) stops at San Felipe. Eventually it is supposed to meet highway 1 at Laguna Chapala.

At Santa Rosalía, 832k/519m, you can take the ferry to Guaymas and continue Route 10 from there. However, it leaves only once a day (11 p.m.), three days a week (Tue, Thur, Sun). The dock from which the ferry leaves is at the south end of town along the highway. Tickets and boarding can be arranged here.

Another choice is from La Paz (1183k/870m) to either Mazatlán (daily) or Topolobampo (Wed, Sat at 8 a.m.). Be forewarned that there is a swamp of bureaucracy to wade through, and unless you know Spanish you may spend hours trying to figure out what to do to get your car on board—if you are lucky, since trucks have preference.

There is an archaeological museum in La Paz on Altamirano and 5 de Mayo streets which reflects the cave dwelling periods of the Baja peninsula (Tue-Sun, 9–1, 4–7).

Appendix 1: Daytrips

Daytrips are round trips from a city where you have chosen to stay overnight or perhaps for several nights. The list that follows presumes that you have your own mobility, although many of the trips can also be made by bus, especially to the larger centers to which trips are more frequent, but much more time will be needed. The cities chosen are on the twelve travel routes. For details, see the Index for the page of a given place or check the route itself. "M" means the place indicated has only a museum. The times are approximations for travel and some sightseeing (time out for eating is extra).

From **Campeche:**
 a) Edzná   3–4 hours
 b) Edzná, Hopelchen, Hochob, Dzibilnococ   8 hours
From **Cancún:**
 a) Tulum   4½ hours
 b) Tulum, Cobá   8 hours
 c) "a" with short stops at Xcaret, Xel-Ha   6 hours
 d) Chichén-Itzá   9 hours
 e) Isla Mujeres
 f) Cozumel
  "e" and "f" depend on departure time and length of stay
From **Guadalajara:**
 a) Los Toriles (Ixtlán del Río)   5 hours
 b) Etzatlán   3 hours
 c) "a" and "b"   7 hours
 d) Autlán   6½ hours
 e) Ciudad Guzmán (M) and Colima (M)   8 hours; returning via Jiquilpan, 10 hours
 f) Teul de González   3–4 hours
From **Manzanillo:**
 a) Autlán 4½ hours; with Barra de Navidad   5 hours
 b) Colima (M) 7 hours; with Ciudad Guzmán 10 hours
From **Mérida:**
 a) Dzibilchaltún   3 hours
 b) Acanceh, Mayapán   4 hours

   c) Uxmal   4–5 hours
   d) Kabah   4 hours
   e) Labná, Xlapak, Sayil   5 hours
   f) "d" and "e"   6½ hours
   g) "c", "d" and "e" above   10 hours
   h) Chichén-Itzá   6 hours
   i) Aké, Izamal, Chichén-Itzá   8 hours
   j) Oxkintok   3–4 hours

From **Mexico City:**
   a) Copilco and Cuicuilco   3 hours
   b) Tlapacoya and Acozac   3½ hours
   c) Huexotla   3½ hours
   d) Texcotzingo   5 hours
   e) "b", "c" and "d"   6 hours
   f) Teotihuacán   8 hours
   g) Ecatepec (M), Tepexpan (M)   4 hours; can be combined with "d" or "f"
   h) Tenayuca and Santa Cecilia   3 hours
   i) Tula   5 hours
   j) Cuernavaca (M), Teoplanzolco   5 hours
   k) Xochicalco   5 hours
   l) "j" and "k"   8 hours
  m) Calixtlahuaca   4 hours
   n) Teotenango, Malinalco   6 hours
   o) "m" and "n"   8 hours
   p) Cacaxtla, Cholula   8 hours
   q) Cacaxtla, Tizapán, Tecoaque, Texcotzingo   10 hours

From **Morelia:**
   a) Tzintzuntzan   3 hours
   b) Pátzcuaro   4 hours
   c) "a" and "b"   4½ hours
   d) with a detour to include Zacapu (M)   6 hours

From **Oaxaca:**
   a) Dainzú, Lambityeco, Yagul, Mitla   6 hours
   b) Monte Albán   4 hours
   c) Zaachila   3 hours

From **Pachuca:**
   a) Huapalcalco   2½ hours
   b) Tepeapulco (M)   2½ hours
   c) Teotihuacán   6 hours
   d) Tula   6 hours

From **Tampico:**
   a) Ciudad Madero   1 hour
   b) Tamuín   3½ hours

   c) Tamuín, Ciudad Valles (M)   5 hours
   d) Tampico Alto (M)   1 hour
   e) Tuxpan (M), Castillo del Teayo   6½ hours

From **Toluca:**
   a) Calixtlahuaca   2 hours
   b) Tenango   3 hours
   c) Malinalco   5 hours
   d) "b" and "c"   6 hours

From **Veracruz:**
   a) Jalapa (M)   4½ hours
   b) Cempoala   3 hours
   c) "a" and "c"   5½ hours
   d) Santiago Tuxtla (M), Tres Zapotes   7 hours
   e) El Tajín   8 hours
   f) "b" and "e"   9 hours

From **Villahermosa:**
   a) Comalcalco   3 hours
   b) Palenque   6 hours

Appendix 2:
Some Motels/Hotels
Along the Way

With one or two exceptions, most guide books discriminate against travelers of modest means and those who travel alone. Tourist brochures likewise tend to accentuate the four- and five-star hotels, and always refer to "double occupancy." Personally, I am satisfied with a simple, clean, comfortable place to spend the night. For people of like mind who travel alone (as I often do) I list here alphabetically for a few of the major cities (and smaller towns along routes where you may have to stay overnight) some of the three and two star hotels found on the Mexican Ministry of Tourism lists, which means they have met at least the basic standards. A lot of hotels you might see or find may not be listed here because they have on-street parking, a definite "no-no." All here have parking facilities (sometimes at nearby enclosed lots). Keep in mind that a three-star hotel in Acapulco is going to be quite a bit more than the same category in Ciudad Victoria. "R" means there is a restaurant; the telephone number of the hotel is given last; the area code follows the city in parentheses.

A word about streets and addresses. Many Mexican cities use the cardinal directions to name their streets, and they are usually abbreviated. Nte is north, Sur is south, Ote (oriente) is east, and Pte (poniente) is west. Some cities like Mérida and Puebla use numbers, with the even numbers running north and south and the odd numbers running east and west. It's a bit confusing at first, but once you catch on to the system, it makes places easy to find.

Acapulco (748) 3*: *Acapulco Imperial*—Costera Miguel Alemán 251, R, 2-29-50; *Bahía*—Gran via Tropical & Aguada, R, 2-01-01; *Bali-Hai*—Costera & Pizarro, R, 4-11-11; *Caleta*—on Caleta beach, R, 2-48-00; *Casino Hornos*—Costera at Hornos beach, R, 4-05-00; *El Matador*—on the hill above Condesa beach, R, 4-32-60. **2***: *Bungalows El Dorado*—Av. Cuauhtémoc 443, 4-05-08; *Caribe*—López Mateos 10, R, 2-15-50; *De Gante*—Costera 265, R, 2-59-60; *Embassy*—Costera 494, R, 4-02-73; *La Jolla*—Costera at López Mateos, R, 2-58-58; *La Riviera*—Costera, 39, R, 2-35-81; *Mallorca*—Gran Via Tropical 28, R, 2-13-75; *Posada del Sol*—Costera 1290, 4-10-10.

Campeche (981) **2***: *América*—Calle 10 #252, 6-45-88; *Campeche*—Calle 57 #2, 6-51-83; *Colonial*—Calle 14 #122, 6-22-22; *El Viajero*—Av. López Mateos #177, 6-51-33; *Posada del Angel*—Calle 12 between Calles 55 and 57, 6-77-18.

Cancún (988) **3***: *Batab*—Av. Chichén-Itzá, R, 4-38-22; *Caribe Internacional*—Av. Yaxchilán & Sunyaxchán, R, 4-39-99; *Caribe Mar*—Av. Kukulkán, R, 3-08-11; *Plaza Caribe*—Av. Uxmal & Tulum 36, R, 3-12-52; *Soberanis*—Cobá 5, 4-30-80; **2***: *Cotty*—Av. Uxmal 48, 4-13-19; *Dos Playas*—Av. Kukulkán, R, 3-04024; *Handall*—Av. Tulum at Cobá, R, 4-11-22; *Novotel*, Av. Tulum 12, R, 4-29-99; *Parador*—Av. Tulum 26, R, 4-19-22.

Chetumal (983) **3***: *Del Prado*—Av. Héroes & Chapultepec, R, 2-05-41; *Rio Hondo*—on highway entering town, R, 2-04-10; *Villanueva*—Carmen Merino 166. **2***: *El Márquez*—Av. Lázaro Cárdenas, R, 2-29-98; *Principe*—Av. Héroes 326, R, 2-47-99; *Real Azteca*—Belice 186, R, 2-07-20.

Chihuahua (14) **3***: *Apollo*—V. Carranza 102, R, 16-11-00; *El Pacifico*—Aldama 1911, 15-07-14; *Nieves*—Av. Tecnológico & Ahuhuetes, R, 13-25-16; *Nuevo Hotel Avenida*—V. Carranza & Juárez, 15-28-91; *Parador San Miguel*—Av. Tecnológico 7901, 17-03-03; *Santa Rita*—Av. Tecnológico 4702, 17-40-47.

Ciudad Victoria (131) **3***: *La Villa Hospedaje*—Matamoros highway; *Paradise Inn*—Matamoros highway k.1, 2-99-88; *Royal*—Aldama & Porfirio Díaz 835, 2-17-71; *Sierra Gorda*—Hidalgo Ote 990, R, 2-22-80. **2***: *Hospedaje Condesa*—8 Hidalgo & Juárez, 2-02-95.

Coatzacoalcos (921) **3***: *Valgrande*—Hidalgo 207, R, 2-16-24. **2***: *Bringas*—Hidalgo 303, 2-10-16; *Casanova*—Av. Morelos 107, 2-00-31; *Colonial*—Zaragoza 417, 2-08-77; *Santa Rosa*—Avila Camacho & Quevedo, 2-05-28.

Colima (331) **3***: *Gran Hotel*—Rey Colimán 18, R, 2-25-25; *Los Candiles*—Camino Real 399, R, 2-32-12. **2***: *Impala*—Independencia & Moctezuma 93, R, 2-15-12.

Córdoba (271) **3***: *Manzur*—Parque 21 de Mayo, R, 2-60-00. **2***: *De Gorbeña*—Calle 11 #308, 2-07-77; *Virreynal*—Av. 1 #309, R, 2-22-35.

Cozumel (987) **3***: *Aguilar*—3 Sur 98, 2-03-07; *Barracuda*—Rafael Melgar, 2-00-02; *Galapagos Inn*—south hotel zone, R, 2-06-63; *Villa Blanca*—Av. Juárez 2bis, R, 2-08-65; *Vista del Mar*—Rafael Melgar 45, R, 2-05-45.

Cuernavaca (73) **3***: *El Verano*—E. Zapata 602, R, 17-06-52; *Irys Astoria*—Pl. del Conquistador 305, R, 13-14-34; *Quinta las Flores*—Tlaquepaque 210, R, 12-62-33. **2***: *El Cid*—E. Zapata 915, 13-04-14; *Los Amates*—Actores 112, R, 13-01-57; *Los Canarios*—Morelos Nte 113, R, 13-44-44; *María Cristina*—A. Obregón 329, R, 12-65-00; *Posada Tlaltenango*—E. Zapata 77, R, 13-70-16; *Suites OK*—E. Zapata 825, R, 13-12-70.

Culiacán (691) **3***: *Cabañas del Rey*—highway 15, k.7 south, 3-56-80; *Fraga*—Hidalgo Pte 227, 2-20-00; *Valle Grande*—Leyva Solano & V. Carranza, 3-92-20. **2***: *Flamingos*—road to Sanalona 9350, 2-88-50; *Francis*—M. Escobedo Pte 135, 2-47-50; *Roma*—H. Colegio Militar 2200, 2-07-81.

Durango (181) **3***: *Campo México Courts*—20 Noviembre Ote 1999, R, 1-55-60; *Durango*—5 de febrero Ote 103, R, 1-55-80; *Nueva Vizcaya*—Parras sur 100, R, 2-44-44; *Paso Real*—5 de Febrero Pte 407, R, 1-33-16; *Reforma*—Madero sur 302, R, 1-31-60. **2***: *Huicot*—B. Martínez Note 165, R, 1-34-50.

Escárcega (981) **2***: *Ah-Kim-Pech*—on highway to VIllahermosa; *María Isabel*—Av. Justo Sierra 127, 4-00-45; *San Luis*—Calle 38 & main plaza, 4-01-10.

Guadalajara (36) **3***: *Metropolitan*—Calzada Independencia sur 278, 14-93-82; *Nueva Galicia*—Av. Corona 610, R, 13-24-58; *Plaza Genova*—Juárez 123, 13-75-00. **2***: *Canadá*—Estadio 77, R, 19-40-14; *Del Bosque*—López Mateos sur 265, R, 21-40-20; *Del Parque*—Av. Juárez 845, 25-42-81; *Guadalajara* Av. Vallarta 3305, 15-57-25; *Posada Guadalajara*—López Mateos 1280, R, 21-20-22; *Universo*—Av. López Cotilla 161, 13-28-25.

Hermosillo (621) **3***: *Bugambilia*—highway 15, north of town, R; *El Encanto*—highway 15, north of town, R.; *La Siesta*—highway 15, north of town.

Isla Mujeres (988) **3***: *Roca Mar*—Av. Nicolás Bravo & Guerrero, R, 2-01-01. **2***: *Caribe Maya*—Av. Madero 9, R, 2-01-90; *Rocas del Caribe*—Av. Madero 2, 2-00-11.

Jalapa (281) **3***: *Posada del Virrey*—Dr. Lucio 142, 8-61-00; *Salmones*—Zaragoza 24, 7-54-31. **2***: *Mexico*—Dr. Lucio 4, 8-80-00.

Mazatlán (678) **3***: *Azteca Inn*—Rodolfo Loaiza 307, 3-44-77; *Del Sol*—Av. del Mar 800. 1-47-12; *Las Brisas*—Av. del Mar 900, 3-66-99; *Los Arcos*—R. Loaiza 214, 3-50-66; *Oasis*—highway 15, 3-09-89; *Sands*—Av. del Mar, 2-00-00. **2***: *Bungalows Damy's*—Av. del Mar & R. Buelna, 3-47-00; *Califaornia*—highway 15 2006, 4-18-09; *San Diego*—Av. del Mar & R. Buelna, 3-57-03; *San Jorge*—Aquiles Serdán 2710, 1-36-45.

Mérida (99) **3***: *Bojorquez*—Calle 58 #483 (at 55), 21-16-16; *Caribe* Calle 59 #500 (at 60), R, 21-92-32; *Colón*—Calle 62 #483 (at 57), 23-43-55; *Del Gobernador*—Calle 59 #535 (at 66), 23-71-33; *Paseo de Montejo*—Calle 56A (at 41), 3-90-33. **2***: *Del Parque*—Calle 60 (at 59), R, 24-78-44; *Nacional*—Calle 61 (at 54), R, 24-92-55; *Posada del Angel*—Calle 67 (66×68), R, 23-27-54; *San Luis*—Calle 68 (at 61), R, 24-76-29.

Mexico City (5) **3***: *Del Angel*—Lerma 154, R, 533-1032; *Majestic*—Madero 73, R, 521-8600; *María Cristina*—Lerma 31, R, 546-9880; *Monte Real*—Revillagigedo 23, R, 518-1149; *Regente*—Paris 19, R, 566-8933; *San Francisco*—Luis Moya 11, R, 521-8960; *Stella Maris*—Sullivan 69,

R, 566-6088; *Vasco de Quiroga*—Londres 15, R, 546-2614. **2***: *Compostela*—Sullivan 35, 535-0733; *Francis*—Reforma 64, R, 566-0266; *Mallorca*—Serapio Rendón 119, R, 566-4833; *Metropol*—Luis Moya 39, R, 510-8660; *Montejo*—Reforma 240, R, 511-9840; *Premier*—Atenas 72, R, 566-2700; *Sevilla*—Serapio Rendón 126, R, 566-1866.

Monterrey (83) **3***: *Colonial*—Hidalgo Ote 475, R, 43-67-91; *El Paso Autel*—Zaragoza Nte 137, R, 41-06-90; *Quinta Avenida*—Madero Pte 243, 75-75-65; *Royalty*—Hidalgo & Carranza, R, 40-98-06; *Son Mar*—Av. Universidad 1211, R, 75-44-00; *Yamallel*—Zaragoza Nte 90, R. 75-35-00. **2***: *Fastos*—Av. Colón Pte 556, 72-32-50; *Jolet*—P. Mier Pte 201, R, 40-55-00; *Los Reyes*—Hidalgo Pte 543, R, 43-61-68; *Nuevo León*—A. Nervo Nte 1007, 74-19-00.

Morelia (451) **3***: *Boulevard*—highway to Salamanca, R, 3-87-35; *Las Américas*—Av. Las Camelinas 2783, R, 4-66-38; *Mansión Acueducto*—Av. Acueducto 25, R, 2-33-01; *Presidente*—A. Serdán 647, R, 2-26-66. **2***: *Mintzícuri*—Vasco de Quiroga 227, R, 2-06-64; *Plaza*—Gómez Farías 278, R, 2-30-95; *Posada Don Vasco*—Vasco de Quiroga 232, R, 2-14-84; *San Miguel*—Madero Pte 1036, R, 2-31-36; *Vallarta*—Madero Pte. 670, 2-40-95.

Oaxaca (951) **3***: *Caleso Real*—García Vigil 306, R, 6-55-44; *Hacienda La Noria*—La Costa 100 at outer loop, R, 6-75-55; *Margarítas*—Madero 1254, R, 6-40-85; *Mesón del Angel*—Mina 518, R, 6-66-66; *Señorial*—Portal de Flores 6, R, 6-39-33. **2***: *Del Arbol*—Calzada Madero 131, R, 6-48-87; *Del Valle*—Díaz Ordaz 208, R, 6-37-07; *Jiménez*—Mier y Terán 213, 6-76-85; *Primavera*—Madero 438, R, 6-45-08; *Santo Tomás*—A. Abasolo 305, R, 6-38-00.

Pachuca (771) **3***: *Emily*—Plaza Independencia, 2-65-17; *San Antonio*—highway 85 to Mexico. **2***: *Hidalgo*—Matamoros 503, 2-59-57; *Los Baños*—Matamoros 205, 2-25-31; *Noriega*—Matamoros 305, 2-01-50; *Plaza El Dorado*—Guerrero 721, 2-52-86.

Pátzcuaro (454) **3***: *Gran Hotel*—Plaza G. Bocanegra 6, R, 2-04-43; *Las Redes*—Av. Las Américas 6, R, 2-12-75; *Mesón del Gallo*—Dr. Coss 20, R, 2-14-74; *Mesón San Miguel*—Plaza Vasco de Quiroga, R, 2-13-13; *Posada de la Basilica*—Arcega 6, R, 2-11-08; *Posada de San Rafael*—Prolongación Vasco de Quiroga, R, 2-07-70. **2***: *Apo-Pao*—Calzada Lázaro Cárdenas, R, 2-06-01; *Posada Imperial*—A. Ogregón 21, R, 2-03-08.

Puebla (22) **3***: *Castillo*—11 Norte 4405, 42-12-48; *Colonial*—4 Sur 105, R, 46-47-09; *Panamericano*—Reforma 2114, R, 48-54-06; *San Leonardo*—2 Oriente 211, R, 46-05-55; *Señorial*—4 Norte 602, R, 44-39-9. **2***: *Cabrera*—10 Oriente 6, R, 42-13-04; *Imperial*—4 Oriente 212, R, 46-38-25; *Virrey de Mendoza*—3 Poniente 912, 42-39-03.

Querétaro (463) **3***: *Azteca*—Constitución 15, R, 2-20-60; *Lisboa*—

Peñuelas 2, 4-53-10; *Impala*—Zaragoza & Corregidora, R, 2-25-70; *Real*—Constitución, k. 3.5, 2-85-19; *Señorial*—Guerrero Nte 10-A, R, 4-37-00. **2***: *Flamingo*—Constituyentes 138, R, 6-20-93; *Gran*—Madero Ote 6, 2-01-24; *María Teresa*—Av. Universidad 306, R, 6-32-26; *San Francisco*—Corregidora sur 144, R, 2-08-58; *Santa Rosa*—Madero 39.

Saltillo (841) **3***: *Estrella*—Blvd. V. Carranga, R, 5-00-11. **2***: *El Paso*— Blvd. Carranga, R, 5-10-35; *Plaza Urdiñola*—Victoria 211, 4-09-40; *Posada San José*—Blvd. V. Carranza, R, 5-23-03; *Premier*—Allende Nte 508, R, 2-10-50.

San Cristóbal de las Casas (967) **3***: *Posada Diego de Mazariegos*—M. A. Flores 2, R, 8-18-25; *Parador Ciudad Real*—Diagonal Centenario 32, R, 8-18-86; *Santa Clara*—Av. Insurgentes 1, 8-11-40. **2***: *Posada Capri*— Insurgentes 54, 8-00-15; *Rincón del Arco*—Ejército Nacional 66, R, 8-13-13.

San Luis Potosí (481) **3***: *Arizona*—J. G. Torres 158, R, 2-65-05; *Concordia*—M. Othón & Morelos, R. 2-06-66; *Filher*—Av. Universidad 375, 2-15-62; *María Cristina*—J. Sarabia 110, R, 2-94-03; *Nápoles*—J. Sarabia 120, R, 4-21-04; *Sands*—highway 57 south of Juárez Circle, R, 2-74-87. **2***: *De Gante*—5 de Mayo 140, R, 2-14-92; *Guadalajara*— Jiménez 253, R, 2-46-12.

Tampico (12) **3***: *Impala*—Díaz Mirón Pte 320, 2-09-90; *Plaza*—Madero Ote 204, 4-16-78; *Posada del Rey*—Madero Ote 218, 4-10-24; *San Antonio Courts*—Hidalgo 3317, R, 3-01-65; *Tampico*—Carranza Ote 513, R, 2-49-70. **2***: *Mundo*—Díaz Mirón Ote 413, 2-05-60.

Tapachula (962) **3***: *San Francisco*—Central Sur 94, 6-14-54. **2***: *Fénix*— 4a Norte 19, 5-07-55; *Gulzar*—4a Norte 27, 6-24-88; *Puebla*—3a Poniente 40, 6-14-36.

Tehuacán (238) **2***: *Iberia*—Av. Independencia 211, R, 2-11-22; *Posada Tehuacán*—A. Camacho 211, 2-04-91.

Tepic (321) **3***: *Corita*—Insurgentes Pte 310, R, 2-04-77; *Ibarra*— Durango Nte 297, 2-38-70; *Villa Las Rosas*—Insurgentes Pte 100, R, 3-18-00. **2***: *Génova*—Zaragoza Nte 51, 2-11-79; *Santa Fe*—Calzada de la Cruz 85, R, 3-010-12.

Ticul (997) **2***: *Conchita*—Calle 21 190, 2-00-29; *San Miguel*—Calle 28; *Cerro Inn*—*Calle 23*, R.

Torreón (17) **3***: *El Paso*—Calzada Interoceanía, R, 13-70-79. **2***: *Arriaga*—Cepeda sur 414, 16-10-55; *Pinguino*—Hidalgo Pte 2310, R, 13-31-44.

Tuxtla Gutiérrez (961) **3***: *Bonampak*—Blvd. Dr. B. Domínguez 180, 3-20-47; *Gran Hotel Humberto*—Av. Central Pte 180, 2-20-44. **2***: *Esponda*—la Pte. Norte 142, 2-00-80; *La Mansión*—la Pte. Norte 221, 2-21-51.

Veracruz (29) **3***: *Guadalajara*—F. J. Mina 1052, R, 2-30-34; *Villa del mar*—Avila Camacho, R, 2-02-27; *Costa Verde*—Avila Camacho 37-97,

R, 7-41-00. **2***: *Mar y Tierra*—General Figueroa & Paseo del Malecón, R, 2-02-60; *Oriente*—M. Lerdo 20, R, 2-01-00; *Real del Mar*—Avila Camacho 2707, R, 7-36-34; *Ruiz Milán*—Paseo del Malecón, R, 2-01-87.
Villahermosa (731) **3***: *Del Parque*—Av. Gregorio Méndez 2911, R, 2-32-13; *Los Arcos*—Madero 207, 2-56-80; *La Paz*—Madero 923, 2-33-62. **2***: *Cristóbal Colón*—Constitución 801, R, 2-33-37; *Ritz*—Madero 1013, R, 2-16-11; *San Rafael*—Constitución 232, R, 2-01-66; *Sofía*—Zaragoza 408, R, 2-60-55; *Tabscoob*—Constitución 508, R, 2-02-11.
Zacatecas (492) **3***: *Del Bosque*—Paseo Díaz Ordaz, R, 2-07-45; *Posada de los Condes*—Juárez 18A, R, 2-10-93; *Posada de la Moneda*—Hidalgo 413, R, 2-08-81; *Reina Cristina*—Hidalgo, R.; *Zacatecas Courts*—López Velarde 602, R, 2-03-28. **2***: *El Convento*—highway 45 to Guadalupe, R, 2-08-49; *La Barranca*—López Mateos 401, R, 2-14-94.

Appendix 3:
A Kilometers-to-Miles Chart

The conversion of kilometers to miles is approximate, not absolutely exact, and is based on one kilometer as equivalent to $5/8$ of a mile.

Km	M	Km	M	Km	M	Km	M	Km	M	Km	M	Km	M
2	1	41	26	81	51	121	76	165	103	290	181	560	350
3	2	43	27	83	52	123	77	170	106	295	184	580	362
5	3	45	28	85	53	125	78	175	109	300	187	600	375
6	4	46	29	86	54	127	79	180	112	310	194	620	387
8	5	48	30	88	55	128	80	185	116	320	200	640	400
10	6	49	31	90	56	130	81	190	119	330	206	660	412
11	7	51	32	91	57	132	82	195	122	340	212	680	425
13	8	53	33	93	58	133	83	200	125	350	219	700	437
14	9	54	34	94	59	134	84	205	128	360	225	720	450
16	10	56	35	96	60	136	85	210	131	370	231	740	462
18	11	58	36	97	61	137	86	215	134	380	237	760	475
19	12	59	37	99	62	139	87	220	137	390	244	780	487
21	13	61	38	101	63	141	88	225	140	400	250	800	500
22	14	62	39	102	64	142	89	230	143	410	256	820	512
24	15	64	40	104	65	144	90	235	147	420	262	840	525
26	16	65	41	105	66	145	91	240	150	430	269	860	537
28	17	67	42	108	67	147	92	245	153	440	275	880	550
29	18	69	43	109	68	149	93	250	156	450	281	900	562
31	19	70	44	110	69	151	94	255	159	460	287	920	575
32	20	72	45	112	70	152	95	260	162	470	294	940	587
33	21	73	46	114	71	155	96	265	165	480	300	960	600
35	22	75	47	115	72	157	97	270	169	490	306	980	612
37	23	77	48	117	73	158	98	275	172	500	312	1000	625
38	24	78	49	118	74	159	99	280	175	520	325	1100	685
40	25	80	50	120	75	160	100	285	178	540	337	1200	750

Index

Entries in *italics* refer to Pre-Hispanic cultures.

About the Author

ROBERT D. WOOD, a Ph.D. in Latin American History, has also long been interested in Anthropology which he taught for ten years at St. Mary's University in San Antonio, Texas, and in archaeology. He established a center for Pre-Columbian studies in Arequipa, Peru, and did archaeological work there. More recently he worked at restoring ruins in Rome. Over a period of twenty years, he has traveled extensively in Mexico, and lived there three years. This book brings together his interests in Mexico, Pre-Columbian history and archaeology. Wood is currently working with Spanish colonial documents in the Academic Library of St. Mary's University, and also in the archives of the Society of Mary (Marianists), St. Louis Province, of which he has been a member for forty-six years.

"Daytrips" travel guides, written or edited by Earl Steinbicker, describe the easiest and most natural way to travel on your own. Each volume in the growing series contains a balanced selection of enjoyable one-day adventures. Some of these are to famous attractions, while others feature little-known discoveries. For every destination there are historical facts, anecdotes, and a suggested do-it-yourself tour, a local map, travel directions, time and weather considerations, food and lodging recommendations, and concise background material.

SOLD AT LEADING BOOKSTORES EVERYWHERE

Or, if your prefer, by mail direct from the publisher. Use the handy coupon below or just jot your choices on a separate piece of paper.

Hastings House
141 Halstead Avenue
Mamaroneck, NY 10543

Please send the following books:

_____copies   DAYTRIPS LONDON @ \$12.95   _____
(0-8038-9329-9)

_____copies   DAYTRIPS IN BRITAIN @ \$12.95   _____
(0-8038-9301-9)

_____copies   DAYTRIPS IN GERMANY @ \$12.95   _____
(0-8038-9327-2)

_____copies   DAYTRIPS IN FRANCE @ \$12.95   _____
(0-8038-9326-4)

_____copies   DAYTRIPS IN HOLLAND, BELGIUM   _____
AND LUXEMBOURG @ \$12.95
(0-8038-9310-8)

_____copies   DAYTRIPS IN ITALY @ \$12.95   _____
(0-8038-9343-4)

_____copies   DAYTRIPS IN EUROPE @ \$15.95   _____
(0-8038-9330-2)

_____copies   DAYTRIPS FROM NEW   _____
YORK @ \$12.95
(0-8038-9332-9)

_____copies   DAYTRIPS TO ARCHAEOLOGICAL   _____
MEXICO @ \$12.95
(0-8038-9336-1)

New York residents add tax: _____

Shipping and handling @ \$1.50 per book: _____

Total amount enclosed (check or money order):   _____

Please ship to: _____

_____

_____